CULTURAL ECOLOGY
Second Edition

Robert M. Netting
University of Arizona

WAVELAND
PRESS, INC.
Prospect Heights, Illinois

For information about this book, write or call:
Waveland Press, Inc.
P.O. Box 400
Prospect Heights, Illinois 60070
(708) 634-0081

Contents

About the Author

Robert M. Netting is Professor of Anthropology at the University of Arizona, Tucson. As an undergraduate at Yale, he majored in English literature; his M.A. and Ph.D. degrees in anthropology are from the University of Chicago. His field research has included a summer on the Ft. Berthold Reservation in North Dakota, three periods totalling 33 months among the Kofyar of Northern Nigeria, and 16 months in the village of Törbel, Valais Canton, Switzerland. This work has been supported at various times by a Ford Foreign Area Studies Fellowship, a Guggenheim Foundation Fellowship, and grants from the Social Science Research Council, the National Science Foundation, and the National Institute of Child Health and Human Development. Concerned primarily with cultural ecology, Netting has written on agricultural practices, household organization, land tenure, warfare, and historical demography. He has collaborated in the use of computer techniques to trace the population dynamics and genealogical lines of a Swiss alpine community over the last 300 years and to measure changes in labor mobilization and food production among Nigerian frontier farmers.

Preface

The brief version of this book was written in 1969-70 at the suggestion of Ward Goodenough; it became part of a series of modular publications designed to present students with a survey of current thinking on individual problem areas in anthropology. The ecological focus and the illustrative ethnographic cases directly reflected undergraduate courses and graduate seminars I had developed during the late sixties at the University of Pennsylvania. At that time ecological anthropology was only beginning to emerge as a recognized subfield in cultural anthropology, and there was a need to indicate its intellectual roots in geography, environmentalist theories, biological models, and the cultural ecology of Julian Steward. The historical development of anthropology has produced a number of classic puzzles or problems on which each new generation of scholars must try their interpretive steel. Hunter-gatherer subsistence, the Northwest Coast potlatch, and the East African cattle complex are among these. By contrasting the ecological approach with more traditional concerns for social structure, values, and personality configurations in the contexts of specific societies, I hoped to emphasize both the potential contributions and the limitations of this viewpoint.

To convey the excitement of research as well as the tentative or preliminary nature of many of the findings, I relied heavily on my own fieldwork experience and on exploring the controversies that were surfacing in the literature. I have not attempted a more generalized and synthetic presentation and critique of ecological theory in anthropology because the task has been so ably assumed by others (Vayda and Rappaport, 1968; Rappaport, 1971a; Vayda and McCay, 1975; Bennett, 1976; Hardesty, 1977; Moran, 1979; Orlove, 1980; Jochim, 1980; Ellen, 1982). "Cultural ecology" is a convenient, conventional title rather than an invitation to scholarly debate, and the topics considered could equally well be included under the headings of ecological anthropology, human adaptation, or cultural geography.

In teaching ecological anthropology, I found that students were often attracted by the "hard data" of a materialist perspective and by the systematic attempt to explain functionally those behaviors that formerly appeared most irrational or exotic. But it was also their skepticism and their probing questions that forced rethinking of many of the ideas expressed here. Student essays, saved over the years, have supplied a wealth of references and taught me a great deal. Indeed, my students at Penn and Arizona—along with my patient informants and my energetic colleagues—are the silent partners of this enterprise, and I owe them more than it is possible to acknowledge. The very nature of ecological investigation demands the crossing of disciplinary lines and asserts a holism often honored but less frequently practiced in anthropology. Archaeologists and physical anthropologists have often understood and adopted an ecological stance with greater alacrity than structuralist or cognitive cultural anthropologists (Netting, 1982b); I see this trend as a healthy one.

Since 1977 when the first paperback edition of *Cultural Ecology* appeared, the amount of ecological research and the number of publications have never stopped growing. Though the work reviewed here was done largely by anthropologists and geographers, it necessarily includes the contributions of agricultural economists, range management specialists, demographers, nutritionists, epidemiologists, and social historians. The journal *Human Ecology* has come out since 1972, and there are now few issues of the *American Ethnologist* or the *American Anthropologist* without papers of ecological interest. Most departments offer sections on ecology and economics in their introductory anthropology courses, and graduate students pursue more specialized studies in the field. The comments of colleagues and students have lead me to think there is still a place for a short non-polemical survey of some problem-oriented ecological case studies. The revised text that Neil Rowe of Waveland Press has encouraged me to prepare includes recent material on hunter-gatherer subsistence, territoriality, and fertility. Ethnographic data on the Northwest Coast has been updated, and there are now more solidly quantitative accounts of African pastoralists. A lively debate has grown up around Boserup's linkage of agricultural change and population pressure, and I have attempted to summarize the positions of both critics and supporters.

My own fieldwork in Switzerland has made me more aware of the complexities of local demographic change and land tenure reconstructed from historic sources. A recent restudy of the Kofyar some twenty-four years after my first visit to Nigeria has demonstrated the potential for rapid voluntary movement from a subsistence to a cash-crop economy without environmental degradation or cultural disintegration. Further studies of intensifying agricultural production on Amazon basin soils and the effects of Green Revolution technology in India suggest the relevance of ecological research to issues of contemporary change and economic policy. One could argue that the methods of ecological analysis represent no genuine advance over the kind of garden-variety functional empiricism that has long characterized much of both biological and social science. But our rigid academic disciplines and narrow professional specializations often hinder a unified approach to the interrelations of natural environment, technology, and human social organization through time. If this book persuades someone of the exciting possibility of providing more adequate approximations of an elusive anthropological reality or arriving at better, if always provisional, answers to the perennial ecological questions, it will have served its purpose.

Robert McC. Netting

Chapter 1

ECOLOGICAL PERSPECTIVES

Ecology is a good, gray scientific term with a respectable derivation from the Greek word *oikos,* meaning "habitation," but it has recently acquired very positive connotations. With popularity and publicity, the term has become more general in usage and less definite in meaning. The biologist Haeckel, who coined the word in 1870, understood ecology to mean

> ... the study of the economy, of the household, of animal organisms. This includes the relationships of animals with both the inorganic and organic environments, above all the beneficial and inimical relations that Darwin referred to as the conditions of the struggle for existence. (Quoted in Bates, 1953)

Though there may be widespread agreement that "ecology deals with organisms in an environment and with the processes that link organism and place," it is also clear that "ecology is not a discipline: there is no body of thought and technique which frames an ecology of man" (Shepard, 1969). It is an approach—a "pervasive point of view rather than a special subject matter" (Bates, 1953).

When cultural anthropologists borrowed the term ecology from the biologists, they also bent it to their own particular uses. They began with humanity, examining the environment as people were affected by it, used it, sought to understand it, and modified it. Their interaction with

1

nature has certainly been humankind's most enduring practical concern, and it may have formed one of their earliest intellectual exercises. Anthropologists have always been aware that the human species is grounded in its environment, but until recent years they have not systematically incorporated this viewpoint in their study. Several factors may account for this avoidance of explicitly ecological formulations. In the first place cultural anthropology, a comparative newcomer with only about 100 years as a separate academic discipline behind it, has necessarily emphasized the particularity and uniqueness of its object of study. Human culture was the focus of anthropology; its understanding could not be left to biologists and psychologists, historians and theologians. Culture was seen as a set of patterns people carried around in their heads that could be investigated quite apart from the study of nature. The natural and the social sciences became specialized and isolated from each other: even when both concentrated on humans they neatly divided them into separate domains, their bodies and their minds. Within anthropology, physical and cultural studies maintained considerable distinctness, and neither related their findings in any consistent way to environmental factors.

In carving out a scholarly sphere of competence, anthropologists also found it necessary to expose the inadequacy of other approaches to human culture. A debunking strain, opposed to simplistic and ethnocentric explanations of cultural differences, has always been strongly evident among anthropologists. With detailed, firsthand information on little-known peoples, they could poke holes in expansive generalizations. Around the turn of the century, a prime target for such efforts was the theory of environmental determinism, which regarded specific cultural characteristics as arising from environmental causes.* Evidently, students of human nature have always been attracted by such explanations. Aristotle noted that "the inhabitants of the colder countries of Europe are brave, but deficient in thought and technical skill, and as a consequence of this they remain free longer than others, but are wanting in political

---

*For a review and criticism of this position by modern geographers, see Thomas (1925, pp. 255ff.) and Sauer (1963, pp. 243-249).

organization and unable to rule their neighbors" (quoted in Tatham, 1951, p. 128). Montesquieu contended that warm climates encourage weakness, timidity, sensitivity to pain, and inordinate sexual indulgences (Thomas, 1925, p. 64). The nineteenth-century anthropogeographer Ratzel claimed that progress was stimulated in regions subject to strong winds and great storms, where the frequent loss of life and property intensified the struggle for existence (see also Huntington, 1963, p. 163). Broad generalizations of this sort were rejected by Kroeber, who insisted that "the immediate causes of cultural phenomena are other cultural phenomena" (1939, p. 1). Anthropologists merely noted the presence of clearly contrasting societies in the same habitat (such as agricultural Hopi pueblos and seminomadic stock-raising Navajo in the Southwest), or pointed out that the islanders of the Torres Straits have lost the art of making canoes though they would benefit by water transportation. "Environment cannot explain culture because the identical environment is consistent with distinct cultures; because cultural traits persist from inertia in an unfavorable environment; because they do not develop where they would be of distinct advantage to a people; and because they may even disappear where one would least expect it on geographical principles" (Lowie, quoted in Thomas, 1925, p. 284).

For the first fifty years of this century, American anthropologists generally subscribed to the "possibilistic" view that environment could permit certain cultural phenomena, but that there were always alternatives and no guarantee that any particular possibility would be the one to materialize.

... the Southwestern Indians did not farm because nature induced them to make the invention. They did not make the invention at all. A faraway people made it, and from them it was transmitted to the Southwest through a series of successive tribal contacts. These contacts, which then are the specific cause of Southwestern agriculture, constitute a human social factor; a cultural or civilizational factor. Climatic or physical environment did not enter into the matter at all, except to render agriculture somewhat difficult in the arid Southwest, though not difficult enough to prevent it. Had the Southwest been thoroughly desert, agriculture could not have got a foothold there. But this would be only a limiting condition; the active or positive causes that brought about the Southwestern agriculture are its invention farther south, the spread of the invention to the north, and its acceptance there. (Kroeber, 1923, p. 185)

This does not mean that anthropologists ignored the influence of climate, topography, and natural vegetation on the groups they studied. Indeed, Wissler (1926) and Kroeber (1939) carefully documented the correspondence between cultural and natural areas in North America. But anthropologists were wary of simple, mechanistic explanations of culture. In making comparisons between societies in generally similar habitats or adjacent regions, they emphasized the complexity of the relationship between the environment and the manifold technical and social devices for exploiting it. "Between the physical environment and human activity there is always a middle term, a collection of specific objectives and values, a body of knowledge and belief: in other words, a cultural pattern" (Forde, 1963, p. 463). The first priority of modern anthropology was to explore culture as embodied by specific societies at particular points in time—to look at it from the inside out in terms of its own patterns and rules. Only thus could a true science of culture be established.

The history of anthropological interest in ecology has been documented in a series of articles and chapters (Helm, 1962; Geertz, 1963, pp. 1-11: Sahlins, 1964; Netting, 1968, pp. 3-25; Vayda and Rappaport, 1968; Damas, 1969b; Anderson, 1974; Netting, 1974; Vayda and McCay, 1975; Bennett, 1976; Orlove, 1980; Ellen, 1982). There is no need to summarize the summaries. Rather it may be helpful to look at cultural ecology as a logical outgrowth of certain tendencies in anthropology, an effort to understand human behavior in a progressively wider and more inclusive frame of reference. At the risk of oversimplifying a complex intellectual development, we might distinguish three major trends in cultural anthropology since 1900. They do not form a clearly defined historical sequence, but rather overlap and interpenetrate. These approaches may be called the ideological, the social structural, and the ecological. When Boas and his students began to single out individual cultures for attention rather than attempting to study human culture as a whole, they focused on a common ideological reality shared in large part by the members of a society. The group was unified by customs, beliefs, and values that formed a patterned and therefore understandable whole. Lacking the history of a primitive group and being unwilling to speculate on the origins of traits, anthropologists searched for internal consistency and meaning. Moreover, the materials of culture could be elicited from individual informants even when, as was often the case with North American Indian groups, the traditional life had been substantially altered. Thus data on shared beliefs (such as religion) and organizational forms (such as kinship) could be collected with relative ease from a small number of informants. This data could then be used to synthesize a picture of culture that related acceptable and predictable behavior, standard material culture, and similar personality characteristics to a common ideology. This ideology resided in the minds of members of the society; it was passed on across the generations and could be analyzed as an entity. An approach of this kind provided excellent descriptions of cultures, but it emphasized group unity over individual differences, norms specifying what should be rather than observations of what is, and what people thought about instead of how they got a livelihood.

With the growing interest in ongoing societies that could be studied intensively in the field by participant observation, anthropological attention shifted from the individual as representative of a cultural tradition to the group whose interaction is socially organized. What was important in culture was seen to lie not in traits of the individual culture bearer but in systematic interaction among members of the group. The focus was still on mental constructs, but these became more specific (rights and duties, roles and statuses) and their operation had to be observed in action as well as described at second hand. The British social anthropologists were less concerned about total configurations of cultural knowledge than about the functional integration of institutions which supported and maintained society. In any social body, as in an organism, the parts had to work together: a discussion of a canoe, for example, necessarily involved the kinship relations of the builders, the political powers of the owner, the magic charms pronounced over it, and the economic purpose of sea travel. The key to the complex, beautiful unity of society was conceived to be its structure, based on kin, marital, and political relations: ". . . social structure is not an aspect of culture but the entire culture of a given people handled in a special frame of theory" (Fortes, 1957). Here were elaborate networks and subtle symmetries to be discovered, whereas subsistence activities were considered simple, undifferentiated, and boringly repetitive wherever one found them.

The tendency to adopt an ecological perspective in anthropological analysis began to gather momentum in the late 1950s and early 1960s (Damas, 1969b, p. 4). This perspective did not arise from conscious adherence to a new theoretical framework or the testing of a defined set of hypotheses. It grew rather from a persistent dissatisfaction with formulations of cultural values and types that were felt to be vague and unprovable, as well as with structuralist interpretations that appeared too rigid to accommodate social change and individual variation. The terms of reference of this new point of view were the broad outlines given by Julian Steward when he defined cultural ecology as the study of "the adaptive processes by which the nature of society and an un-predictable number of features of culture are affected by the basic adjustment through which man utilizes a given environment" (Tax, 1953, p. 243). Through empirical analysis, a "cultural core" of features most closely related to subsistence activities and economic arrangements was to be specified (Steward, 1955, p. 37). Chiefly it was the experi-ence of fieldwork that convinced younger anthropologists that the pro-cesses of human adaptation to the environment had been undervalued and that sound empirical data, some of them quantifiable, were available to document wide-ranging and systematic ecological relationships. The excitement was not that of overthrowing old ideas, but of putting them in a more inclusive context. Functionalism was extended beyond the social sphere, structural arrangements were seen to have adaptive value in organization for defense and production, cultural attitudes showed selective advantages in promoting subsistence success. The ability of another set of facts to help make sense of what is already known by pointing out further order and meaning is, after all, at the heart of scientific endeavor.

If cultural ecology were a little older, rather less diverse, and not so lively, it might be possible to develop a connected theoretical and methodological summary in the following pages. I believe that such an overview is premature—we are too busy dealing with the details of specific subsistence systems, instances of micro-evolution, and limited regional comparisons to begin the process of definition and synthesis characteristic of a more mature discipline. There is only one way to explain what cultural ecology is: to show what it is doing. Whatever unity the approach has is evident when its findings are contrasted with those resulting from other anthropological attempts to deal with the same data. For this reason I have selected several perennial questions and widely accepted impressions of primitive peoples for reevaluation from an ecological point of view. Most beginning students of cultural anthropology quickly become familiar with hunter-gatherer "hardships," the "excesses" of Northwest Coast potlatching, the East African's "love for his cows," and the "uneconomic," "conservative" practices of most preliterate farmers. This book will contrast the ways these institutions and attitudes have been characterized and explained in the past with their more recent treatment in the writings of ecologically-oriented anthropologists. In so doing, we will follow the time-honored practice of postponing any general theory of behavior, offering "case studies" instead. This effort relies heavily on very new publications by a variety of students. In combining the work of many, we may well miss important contributions or mistake the intent of some passages. Yet it seems timely to provide at least an interim report on an ecological "way of seeing" that has gained some currency in modern cultural anthropology.

Chapter 2

HUNTER-GATHERERS

Of all the peoples studied by anthropologists, hunter-gatherers are the most likely to be considered in ecological terms. Their relationship to their physical environment is so direct, since they depend on naturally occurring plants and animals for daily food, that it seemed obvious to view subsistence techniques as largely conditioning their way of life. Moreover, the tools and methods of exploitation of such peoples are usually simple, providing little opportunity for food accumulation and storage and scant protection from the elements. Those archetypal hunters, the Eskimos, were among the first subjects of ecological investigation by modern anthropologists. Boas (1888) demonstrated a relationship among sea-ice conditions, the presence of seal that could effectively be hunted, and Eskimo population concentration. The change of seasons altered both subsistence possibilities and the size of the Eskimo settlement group that could most effectively utilize them (Mauss and Beuchat, 1905). After such sound pioneering studies, it is remarkable that most subsequent work on hunter-gatherers ignored the empirical consideration of livelihood as related to habitat in favor of perpetuating a series of doubtful stereotypes.

The shift of interest from people in their environment to a more limited view of culture as an ideological or mentalistic phenomenon was evident in the early career of Franz Boas, whose intellectual direction so strongly influenced the first generation of American academic anthropologists. As an outgrowth of his German university studies in psychophysics, Boas had developed a strong bent toward human geography. He planned to study the relationship among the migration of Eskimos, their perception of their surroundings, and the actual topography of the land. He himself measured the configurations of the local Baffin-land terrain and then asked Eskimos to draw maps and describe their travels. Though some of this material was incorporated in later publications, Boas came to feel that "immediate environmental influences were 'patent' and the study was too 'shallow to illuminate the driving forces that motivate behavior' " (Stocking, 1968, p. 151). The simple case of geography modifying culture he had hoped to find in the Arctic turned out to be extremely complex and to neglect the distinctive psychological character of the people (Stocking, 1968, p. 153). It was the "mind of primitive man" that interested Boas, and although the environment was involved in both the artifacts of daily life and the development of beliefs and theories, the crucial factors shaping cultural individuality and uniqueness were predominantly intellectual (Thomas, 1925, p. 277).

PRIVATION OR ABUNDANCE?

Until recently, the most common picture of hunter-gatherers was that of an uncertain existence in a harsh environment with limited and primitive technology. People who did not plant and harvest and who kept no domestic animals were thought to be at the mercy of an unpredictable climate, threatened with starvation and working constantly to achieve bare survival. Their social organization was similarly simple and restricted, based on a group of male relatives who brought their wives from similar small neighboring groups and moved about a territory that they owned and defended. This view was perhaps more projection than description. It was based in part on our tendency to pigeonhole human groups in some evolutionary framework. Any society of tiny wandering aggregations with nothing more sophisticated than bows, spears, and clubs must be at the opposite extreme from our huge, sedentary, highly organized, technologically complex Western culture. If we were rich, they were poor; if we lived long, they died early; if we had abundance, they never knew where their next meal was coming from. If our civilization was based on leisure, they, who lacked writing, temples, and slaves, had obviously not had the spare time to develop such things. This characterization not only felt right in terms of our own experience, but it also persisted because no one wanted to share the hard nomadic life of these people long enough to understand it. The soldiers and travelers who briefly encountered hunter-gatherers in deserts or mountains merely supported this view. The Shoshoni Indians of the Great Basin were said to live in single families, without firearms, eating seeds and insects and digging roots, providing nothing for future wants, living like animals and representing humanity in its lowest form and its most elementary state (statements of Fremont, Leonard, and Farnham quoted in Steward, 1938). Field research during the last twenty-five years has demolished the self-serving myth of hunter-gatherer struggle for existence. We now have such basic information as what and how much hunter-gatherers eat, how long they work to get it, when and why they move, and what their life span is. In the process of gathering these data, a rich variety of forms of social organization have been disclosed and their adaptive value suggested. Statements of these principles of adaptation and abundant ethnographic evidence were first assembled in the volume *Man the Hunter* (Lee and DeVore, 1968); the summary that follows takes up these issues in the light of more recent data and lively scholarly debates.

Most important is the fact that, far from being pressed to the wall by want and unavailing exertion, hunter-gatherers (1) have a food base that is with minor exceptions adequate and reliable; (2) expend minimal labor to provide for their physical needs; and (3) live often to a ripe old age with few signs of anxiety or insecurity. Outside the Arctic wastes, most hunters depend to a large degree on vegetable products. The unpredictability of hunting even where game is plentiful necessitates a major emphasis on dependable botanical sources. Even in the semiarid Kalahari Desert of Botswana, such plant foods are locally plentiful and easily collected during most of the year. Richard Lee (1968; 1969; 1979), whose careful ecological inquiries among the !Kung San (formerly known as Bushmen) have broken new ground, has shown that nuts, roots, fruit, melons, and berries make up 60 to 80 percent by weight of the annual diet. In fact, 28 percent of San food intake in the group examined was composed of protein-rich mongongo nuts (Lee 1979, p. 270). The nut groves are quite extensive and apparently dependable, with total annual production for the Dobe area estimated at 325 million calories (Lee, 1973). Edible nuts may be gathered from the ground up to a year after they have fallen, and the present San population does not exploit the entire available yield. An average daily adult consumption of 300 nuts supplies the same number of calories as 2.5 pounds of cooked rice and the protein equivalent of 14 ounces of lean beef (Lee, 1968, p. 33). Foods may change with the season, but San select only the tastiest and most easily collected from a wide range of plants known and available to them. The diet, including an average 4 ounces of meat daily per person, yields some 2355 calories (Lee, 1979, p. 271), which appears sufficient to prevent nutritional deficiencies as well as to exceed average San energy requirements (Lee, 1969, p. 90). Like other collectors-who-also-hunt (Stewart, 1938), the San have such a wide and precise knowledge of their environment and its seasonal opportunities that little-exploited types of food almost always exist to fall back on. Thus San continue to be well fed when Bantu pastoralists sharing the same environment are experiencing serious scarcity (Lee, 1968, p. 40). Not all environments provide the San with the same food resources. The G/wi in central Botswana don't have a reliable staple like the mongongo, and they must compensate for a lack of permanent water holes by consuming six to eight pounds of tsama melons (Figs. 2a and 2b) and other esculent plants daily (Silberbauer, 1972). The Hadza of Tanzania are better protected from famine than their agricultural neighbors because the bush plants on which they rely are highly regular in yield, quite diverse, and less vulnerable than cultivated crops to drought, insects, and birds (Woodburn, 1968). There is no doubt that hunter-gatherers may at times go hungry, but available evidence suggests that only such specialized hunting groups as Eskimos and boreal forest Indians, subject to extreme weather conditions and limited in variety of food resources, run the risk of starvation. The long-term evolutionary success of this adaptation, which has fostered man for 99 percent of his career as a culture bearer, argues for the sufficiency and security of hunting and gathering in fulfilling human needs (Lee and DeVore, 1968, p. 3).

As a mode of life support, hunting and gathering appears to be not only effective but remarkably efficient. Although few periods are entirely free of subsistence activity, the ratio of labor expenditure to production is very favorable. Hunter-gatherers are quite literally "the most leisured peoples in the world" (Service, 1966, p. 13); Sahlins has called them "the original affluent society" (Lee and DeVore, 1968, p. 65). Observations such as these, which run counter to the received opinions of the past, are based on the simple expedient of keeping diary records of labor time over defined periods. The necessities of the food quest clearly do not dominate the lives of such people as the Hadza, who "meet their nutritional needs easily, without much effort, much forethought, much equipment, or much organization" (Woodburn, 1968). During the dry season men are able to spend more time gambling than hunting, and some men almost never kill large game. In one 28-day period, adult San spent an average of 2.4 work days per week in subsistence activities (Lee, 1979, p. 256). A woman can gather enough in one day to feed her family for three, leaving her plenty of time for resting, visiting, doing embroidery, and entertaining visitors (Lee, 1968, p. 37). Even when the time spent in making and repairing tools, clothing, and shelters, plus that required for household tasks, such as nut cracking, butchery, cooking, and firewood collecting, are added to time devoted to gathering and hunting, the average adult San work week is only 42.3 hours (Lee, 1979, pp. 272-280). Though men work about 4½ hours more per week than women, this does not include the time spent on child care by mothers (Lee, 1979, p. 280). Men devote a significant proportion of time to ritual trance dances. Though the Kalahari impresses outsiders with its barrenness, the !Kung food quest does not even approach the forty-hour week that is a customary standard in modern societies. Observations by McCarthy and McArthur of Australian aborigine labor expenditure in gathering and preparing food over a three-week period give an average time of four to five hours per day per person in an undemanding and highly intermittent subsistence quest (Sahlins, 1972, pp. 14-20). In light of such facts, one wonders whether the myth of hunter-gatherer hardships might not have been propagated over the centuries in part to convince farmers and craftsmen to work longer and more arduous days and thus to support denser populations and more complex societies.

The precarious existence of hunter-gatherers is further belied by the composition of the population. Some 10 percent of the 466 people surveyed by Lee were more than 60 years old, "a proportion that com-

pares favorably to the percentage of elderly in industrialized populations" (Lee, 1968, p. 36). Those who are blind, senile, or crippled
continue to be supported. Young and aged are both relatively unproductive, and yet they constitute about 40 percent of the population of
most camps.

BAND FLEXIBILITY

The same impulse that encouraged collection of more accurate data on
hunter-gatherer subsistence systems and work routines also led to more
detailed analyses of social organization. Here the emphasis has been on
breaking down the stereotype of self-contained patrilocal band or
horde with an exclusive territory and substituting for it a clear description of existing, highly fluid social units with obvious adaptive value.
Steward's work, which began to appear in 1936, used American Indian
and other groups to show a number of levels of sociocultural integration among hunter-gatherers and to discuss the detailed ecological
relationships of each (this material is summarized in Steward, 1955,
Chapters 6, 7, and 8). The family was the principal social unit of the
Ute, Western Shoshoni, and Northern Paiute peoples of western Colo-
rado, Utah, Nevada, and eastern Oregon and California. Because of the
dryness of the Great Basin and the Plateau, food resources—especially
seed-bearing grasses—were sparse, widely spaced, and unpredictable.
Population had to be similarly dispersed and mobile, with minimal
independent units for food getting. Peoples living in somewhat larger
groups, which Steward called patrilineal bands, also had a limited technology and scattered food resources, but they depended on game that
could be hunted collectively. Since this game occurred only in small,
nonmigratory groups, it would not support large aggregations of
people. Men, as hunters, appeared to have greater economic importance, and it made sense for men to remain in the area in which they
had grown up, where their intimate knowledge of the territory increased their chances of finding game. Such males, therefore, tended
to remain in a defined territory and form the core of a patrilineally
related, patrilocal group. Steward believed that Bushmen, Congo
Pygmies, Australian aborigines, and others represented this level. Where
large game herds were prevalent, hunters-and-gatherers could assemble

in bigger groups called composite bands, consisting of many unrelated nuclear families; these were found among the Algonkian and Athabaskan Indians of Canada.

Steward's insights into ecological relationships have proved amazingly stimulating, but the ethnographic data on which they were based were often incomplete (Barnard, 1983). On the basis of the increased information gathered from longer periods of participant observation, the collection of quantitative material, and especially the mining of historical sources, the organization of hunter-gatherer bands now appears to be extremely flexible. The reality of adjustment to changing environmental demands resists any clearly defined typology. Steward himself recognized that with the introduction of the horse and the entrance of whites into their country, some family-level Shoshoni rapidly developed multi-family, mounted, predatory bands (Steward, 1955, p. 121). Similarly, the more reliable and productive resources of the Owens Valley in California allowed Paiute bands there to form permanent villages with ownership of land, direction of chiefs, and some tendency to matrilineal organization (Steward, 1938, pp. 50-52; 1955; p. 108). More recently, Steward (1968) has come to the view that isolated nuclear families are very exceptional, and that clusters of several families, frequently numbering around twenty-five individuals and forming a ''primary band,'' are more typical of the Western Shoshoni, San and Australians. Within and among such groups, however, there is ''great seasonal variation and change over periods of years.''

The fluidity of local group composition among hunter-gatherers is obviously correlated with environment and the size of the human group utilizing it. A movement of people, either temporary or permanent, from one primary band or camp to another is a quick way of adjusting group size to available resources, whether changes arise from local abundance or scarcity of food or from demographic variance among groups. At the same time, the spatial shifts of any one group may be interpreted in terms of seasonal subsistence opportunities. Both personnel changeover and nomadic movements have been grouped together as "flux" (Turnbull, 1968, p. 132). Among the hunters of the Great Plains, a regular seasonal pattern of summer tribal aggregation for the great hunt and winter splitting into smaller composite bands mirrored the annual aggregation of the bison into large herds and subsequent dispersion of the animals into more sheltered pastures. This pattern provided the advantages both of cooperative hunting on horse-back and of exploitation of nonherding animals in the limited areas in which fuel and protection from winter storms were more adequate (Oliver, 1962). In such a situation, maintenance of groups rigidly structured by kinship would have been in conflict with the needs for seeking out the best areas for winter camps and for attaching indi-vidual families to successful military leaders.

The circulation of individuals among Bushman camps has both short-term and long-term aspects. A camp changes in size and composition from day to day (Lee, 1968, p. 31). Over one 28-day period, a single camp was observed to vary from twenty-three to forty persons (Lee, 1969, p. 85). There are no social rules for permanent group member-ship, and "the camp does not constitute in any way a patrilocal band" (Lee and DeVore, 1968, p. 132). The requirement of bride service also redistributes population. After marriage, the husband joins his wife's group, ostensibly to provide meat for his new in-laws and give them a chance to judge his character. The duration of this residence is indefi-nite, but a husband should stay long enough for three children to be born, which may be ten years or more. Thus, although men say that they derive a certain benefit from hunting in the area in which they grew up, half of all adult men appear to be living with their wives' groups (Marshall, 1960). Easy movement between groups of hunter-gatherers is often facilitated by customs such as name sharing, according to which one can address the relatives of anyone with whom one shares a name by the same kinship terms used by the namesake. When the total number of names in the society is limited and names are often repeated, as among Bushmen (Marshall, 1957) or some Eskimo groups (Guemple, 1965), this device significantly extends the number of individuals with whom one may exercise some of the rights and duties of kinship. A similar effect is achieved by Mbuti Pygmies, who extend their generational kinship terminology to nonrelated persons in the band, simply including them on the basis of age in the appropriate generation of established kin (Turnbull, 1965, p. 292). Indeed, both local bands and regional groupings of bands sharing a common territory and social identity are characterized by a range of kinship ties. Helm (1968) found that throughout a fifty-year time span, every resident of a Canadian Dogrib regional band had one or more primary consanguines (siblings and/or parents) in the band or was married to an already consanguineally linked member of the band. These "bilateral primary linkages" provided each married pair with several residence alternatives.

Ecological studies sometimes overlook the fact that the relationship of organisms to their environment also includes the relationships of individuals of the same species to one another. Among hunter-gatherers, the fission and recombination of camp groups not only improves subsistence opportunities but also helps in dealing with interpersonal friction. These two factors are not unrelated; situations of declining hunting catches or vegetable food yields may stimulate disagreements and ill feeling. People often trace the breakup of a camp or band explicitly to quarreling or fights. We are just becoming able to suggest that ecological contexts may affect the way in which human "cussedness" is expressed. Mbuti Pygmies of the Ituri Forest in eastern Zaire live most of the year in groups whose size is dependent on two contrasting hunting techniques. Those who drive game into a semicircle of connected nets require at least seven families with nets for effective coverage of a circle 100 yards in diameter. With more than thirty families, however, a much larger area would have to be included and the drive would be difficult to coordinate and control (Turnbull, 1965, p. 298). Archer groups, on the other hand, rely much less on cooperation. Men go singly or in groups of three or four to lie in wait near game trails and shoot animals brought within range by game calls or flushed by dogs Bicchieri, 1969). Though it was once thought that there was no environmental reason for the division into net hunters and archers (Turnbull, 1968, p. 134; Bicchieri, 1969, p. 68), the forest is not a uniform habitat. Net hunters live in the less disturbed western part of the Ituri, while archers are found to the east, where game is scarcer because of the presence of more shifting cultivators, commercial plantations, and administrative settlements (Abruzzi, 1980, p. 11). Garden crops traded for meat and forest products may be more important to the Mbuti under these circumstances, and they leave the neighborhood of the villages and search out wild honey only during the "hungry season" when crops have not yet been harvested and food is in limited supply. Archers, whose usual mode of dependence on settled agriculturalists and sparse game keeps them in small, fragmented groups, return briefly to the forest and assemble in larger camps for communal hunting. The fission into smaller camps of the net hunters during the same rainy months of April through June (Turnbull, 1983, p. 39) may be due both to a seasonal reliance on honey which can be collected without collective effort and to the desire to avoid conflict built up within the cooperative group.

Because people are social creatures, wanting company and yet often in conflict, the movements of families and the flexibility of band membership is not a direct reflection of environmental imperatives. Hunter-gatherers may circulate for social reasons, even when immediate needs for vegetable foods, water, and hunting cooperation are being met. San are brought together near dry-season water holes by necessary concentration and by the desire for more intensive interaction. They value occasions when dancing, curing, trading, initiation, and marriage arrangement may take place. But what Lee (1972b) calls the increased "social velocity" also raises the potential of conflict among the "harmless people." Fifteen of eighteen recorded murders took place in camps of more than forty people. The most common social response to such violence or its threat is to split the group into more comfortable bands of twenty or so. Fission is thus not necessarily a response to food scarcity but may operate to cause dispersion and prevent enduring population aggregations.

If sociability is desired but parting company is the easiest way to relax social tensions, mobility may be considerably greater than that required for the subsistence quest. The Hare Indians of the Canadian boreal forest undergo environmental stress during the winter trapping season, when they live as dispersed family units dependent on unstable food resources and the vagaries of a severe climate. Social isolation and enforced cooperation create tensions within the small groups. Yet seasonal concentration of population at the trading post brings arguments over divisions of food and loans of equipment as well as the potential danger of social drinking and fighting. A pendulumlike movement from bush to settlement and back again thus appears as a stress-reducing and conflict-avoiding mechanism (Savishinsky, 1971).

POPULATION CONTROL

One aspect of the emerging picture of hunter-gatherers as existing in a stable, secure, and relatively benign relationship with the environment

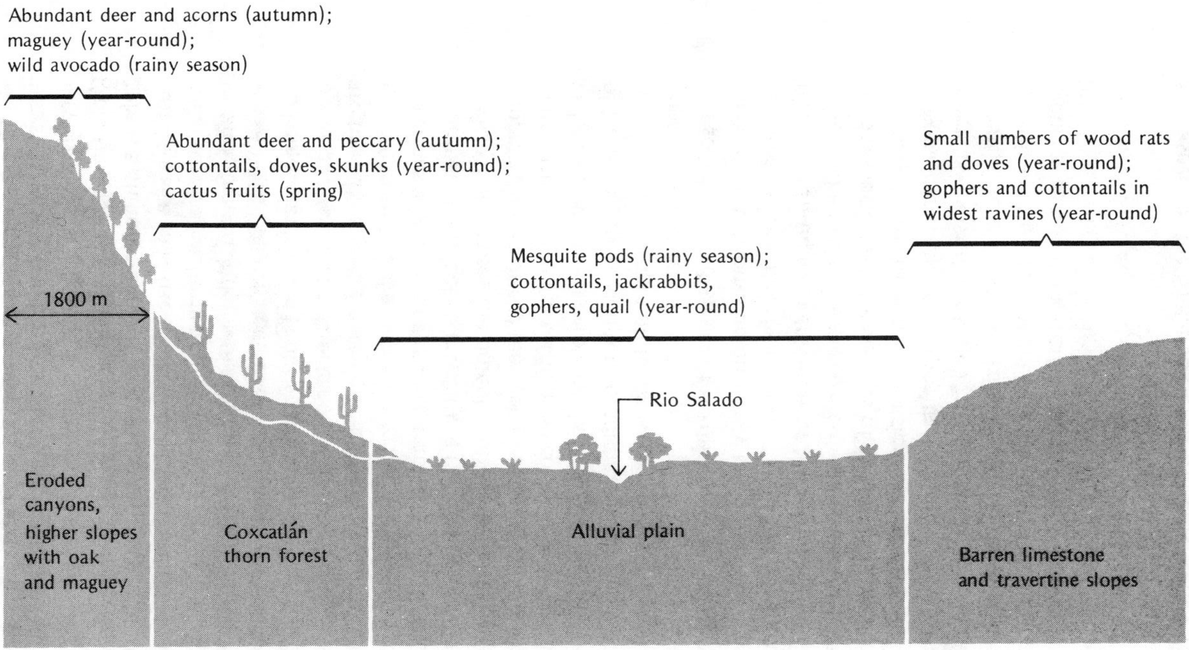

Abundant deer and acorns (autumn); maguey (year-round); wild avocado (rainy season)

1800 m

Eroded canyons, higher slopes with oak and maguey

Abundant deer and peccary (autumn); cottontails, doves, skunks (year-round); cactus fruits (spring)

Coxcatlán thorn forest

Mesquite pods (rainy season); cottontails, jackrabbits, gophers, quail (year-round)

Alluvial plain

Rio Salado

Small numbers of wood rats and doves (year-round); gophers and cottontails in widest ravines (year-round)

Barren limestone and travertine slopes

Figure 1. *Microenvironmental zones of the Tehuacan Valley, Puebla, Mexico. Archaeological research has shown the seasonal exploitation of various subsistence resources by bands of prehistoric hunter-gatherers. By moving their camps and choosing among alternative foods, the Indians avoided permanent depletion of the various plants and animals on which they depended. (Redrawn from Figure 1 in Michael D. Coe and Kent V. Flannery, "Microenvironments and Mesoamerican Prehistory," Science 143(3607): 650-654, 1964. Copyright © 1964 by the American Association for the Advancement of Science.)*

has been the postulate that their numbers are regulated well below carrying capacity. Food resources appear adequate even during periods of climatic adversity, continuous subsistence effort is not required, and there is little evidence of intense competition for hunting or gathering areas. Groups may use limited microenvironments in several adjoining zones, seasonally altering both their food procurement system and the size and composition of the coresident group. On the basis of a long archaeological sequence in the Tehuacan valley, Flannery (1968) has shown how prehistoric bands sought maguey plants year-round in the high arid valleys and cactus fruit and leaves in the thorn forests during the spring (Fig. 1). Mesquite pods were gathered on the alluvial plains during the rainy season and herding deer harvested from the hills in the autumn. Cottontail rabbits were hunted year-round with snares and throwing sticks. Among resources with a seasonal occurrence those which were most abundant and accessible could be chosen. Procurement schedules could be changed and groups could fragment or coalesce. Such alternatives diminished pressure on declining resources, allowing them to recover, and maintained a generalized equilibrium of human beings in relation to their environment.

Such a steady state could endure only if demographic fluctuation was limited. Indeed, archaeologists have often taken as axiomatic that once adapted to their environment, prehistoric hunter-gatherer populations tended to remain stable at densities below the point of resource exhaustion (Binford, 1968). Living groups of San and Australian aborigines are similarly said to utilize only some of the resources available to them and to show no evidence of population expansion. The means by which growth is controlled are less clear. Disease and outright famine are thought to be relatively unimportant, whereas social means such as prolonged nursing, abortion, infanticide, and abstention from sexual intercourse have been cited as probable methods (Lee and DeVore, 1968, pp. 241-243). Lee noted that long-term population growth among nomadic San appeared to be only 0.5 percent a year, and the birth interval between living children was approximately four years. The total average number of live births for San women of age 45 and over was only 4.6, one of the lowest fertility rates known for any society that does not practice birth control (Howell, 1979, pp. 125, 155). He speculated that the added burden of carrying more than one infant on gathering trips was enough to discourage women from bearing a child before the previous one could walk (Lee, 1972a). Once San shifted to a sedentary life partially dependent on agriculture and dairying, the birth interval of 44 months declined by 18 percent (Lee 1979, p. 322). Not only was carrying infants less difficult for the mother because of food sources closer to home, but the availability of soft foods such as milk and cooked grains allowed infants to be weaned earlier (Kolata, 1974). Long lactation is now generally believed to inhibit fertility by lengthening the birth interval (Solien de Gonzalez, 1964; Jain, et al., 1970; Daly and Wilson, 1978, p. 284; Harrell, 1981). If a certain minimum proportion of body fat is needed for ovulation (Frisch, 1975), the drain of 1000 calories a day on a lactating woman plus the expenditure of more energy in the food quest might delay conception. Many !Kung women, however, become pregnant again before they reach the level of critical fatness (Howell, 1979, pp. 189-211). The biochemical mechanism actually involved appears to be the release of prolactin into the maternal system, stimulated by the infant's sucking on the nipple. San mothers nurse briefly and at average intervals of 13 minutes, causing the release of gonadal hormones that maintain milk secretion and promote infertility (Konner and Worthman, 1980). Improvement of the nutritional status of the mother and substitution of other foods for breast milk in the child's diet would decrease the frequency of nursing, potentially raising hunter-gatherer fertility and contributing to population pressure.

There is cross-cultural evidence that prolonged lactation lengthens postpartum amenorrhea, the time between birth and the resumption of menstruation. Surveys of Taiwanese mothers who breastfed infants an average of sixteen months showed a mean of eleven months of post-partum amenorrhea (Jain et al., 1970). In Bangladesh, where maternal malnutrition is prevalent, the median length of amenorrhea for women with a surviving breastfed child is about seventeen months. This period is significantly reduced if supplemental food is given to the child, and women who did not nurse at all began to menstruate again only two months after pregnancy (Chen, Ahmed, and Mosley, 1974). Because both San food intake and work effort may fluctuate seasonally, there may be fewer conceptions. Wilmsen (1978) has found annual cycles of hormonal change and low conception among San during the dry season, and this apparently reduced overall fertility. Lee (1979, pp. 304-306), on the other hand, contends that the more mobile foragers show minimal weight loss and are not subject to periodic failure of wild resources. In contrast, the healthy and well-nourished Hutterites of North America, despite nearly universal maternal lactation, have an estimated mean postpartum amenorrhea of six months (Sheps, cited in Chen, Ahmed, and Mosley, 1974). These studies might suggest that even a generally adequate hunter-gatherer diet is insufficient to permit rapid resumption of ovulation when both heavy nursing by mothers and strenuous food collection and infant transportation efforts are required (Howell, 1976). The relationship of birth spacing and fertility to health and nutrition is obviously significant for population stability or growth, but we are only beginning to understand it.

Though it is tempting to contrast an elegantly adjusted system of zero population growth among hunter-gatherers with the rapidly pro-liferating hordes of all other world societies, the evidence is by no means conclusive. We lack reliable information on the size and age structure of such populations over even three or four generations. In addition, it is very difficult to formulate a measurable physical corre-late for concepts of carrying capacity that biologists use only in certain restricted contexts (Ammerman, 1975; Brush, 1975; Hayden, 1975). The problem of identifying all plant and animal resources, for example, is complicated by the fact that all human populations have likes and dislikes in food consumption, that their systems of exploitation may change, and that the effect of maximum resource use may be to lower the total potential of the environment. Small natural populations of animals tend to fluctuate because of chance factors in birth and death, variations in the environment, and cycles in related populations of predator and prey (Ammerman, 1975). Rather than showing a neat homeostatic relationship to a relatively stable habitat, local hunter-gatherer populations may have undergone considerable oscillation in numbers, alternately overshooting and falling below the levels of the food supply (Vayda and McCay, 1975; Bennett, 1976, pp. 168-190). The systematic interaction of population size with environment, as influenced by resource availability, technology, human biology, and cultural self-regulation (abortion, infanticide, war-fare, migration, and so on) has been modelled only in a crude and incom-plete way by scientific investigators. We have learned just enough to say that inclusive statements of equilibrium or mere random fluctuation cannot do justice to the complexity of real ecosystems.

TERRITORIALITY

The question of whether hunter-gatherer groups have bounded, defended territories to which they claim exclusive exploitation rights is still
a thorny issue among anthropologists. Steward (1938) identified Paiute
groups with particular areas such as Death Valley and located the campsites and resources they customarily used, but he made it clear that
bands moved freely into each other's home range to take advantage of
abundant piñon nut supplies, to cooperate in antelope drives, or to
escape the effects of drought. Because of the erratic annual and local
occurrence of foods, the arbitrary exclusion of territorially delimited
groups of families from utilization of other territories would have
caused starvation and death (Steward, 1955, p. 108). The flexibility of
!Kung San camps suggests a similar lack of clearly defined property rights
to land. Yet a report on the G/wi San of central Botswana (Silberbauer,
1972) contends that each band of twenty-one to eighty-five members
has exclusive rights to the exploitation of a "resource nexus" consisting
of fruits, melons, seeds, leaves, and nuts in territories of 200 to 400
square miles with no permanent water supplies. The band moves as a
single or "synoecious" community to eight or ten different campsites
over the period December to July and divides into dispersed nuclear or
small extended families for the remaining four months (Fig. 2). The !Kung
San have well developed concepts of owner and territory (n!ore) with
rights coming through either parent and strongly held rights where one is
resident plus residual or weakly held rights in the territory identified with
the other parent. A group of kin collectively own and inherit a water
hole and scattered resources such as mongongo nut groves and wild
bean patches, but broad belts of foraging land are shared with adjacent
groups. Immigrants who join and stay with a group are generally
absorbed into the core identified as owners (Lee, 1979, pp. 333-369).

   Territoriality, as considered in biological and ethological studies, may
result from intraspecific aggression or from attachment to a site or
area. Neither presupposes the other, and either may lead to the orderly
spacing that controls population and approximates an optimum density
(Peterson, 1975). Biological ecologists have developed a cost-benefit
model of economic defendability according to which "territorial behavior
is expected when the cost of exclusive use and defense of an area are
outweighed by the benefits gained from this pattern of resource

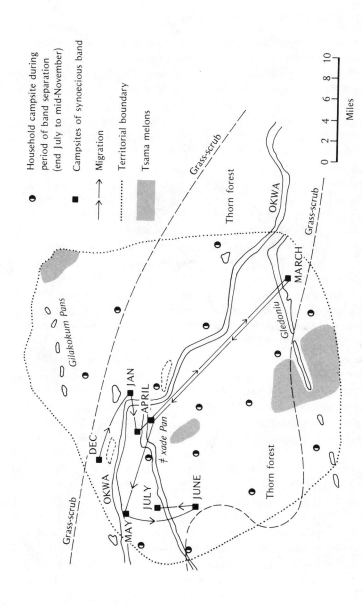

Figure 2a. *Band and household migration. Migration in ≠ Xade territory during a year of poor tsama season.* (From "The G/wi Bushmen," in George Silberbauer, Hunters and Gatherers Today, edited by M.G. Bicchieri. Copyright © 1972 by Holt, Rinehart and Winston, Inc. Redrawn by permission of Holt, Rinehart and Winston.)

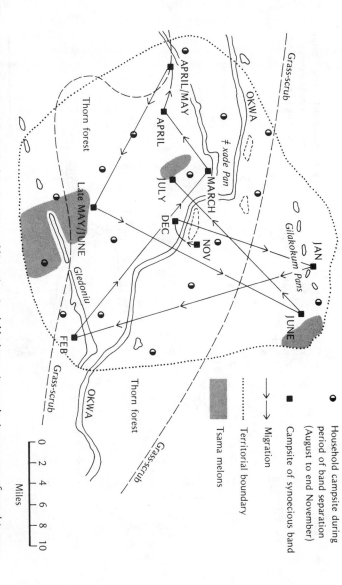

Figure 2b. *Band and household migration. Migration in ≠Xade territory during a year of good tsama season. (From "The G/wi Bushmen," in George Silberbauer, Hunters and Gatherers Today, edited by M.G. Bicchieri. Copyright © 1972 by Holt, Rinehart and Winston, Inc. Redrawn by permission of Holt, Rinehart and Winston.)*

utilization" (Dyson-Hudson and Smith, 1978, p. 23). When resources are abundant or dense at particular locations and at times of the year that are predictable, it may be useful to establish and defend some continuing claim to them. If the time, energy, and risk required to enforce this claim are too great (imagine a hunter-gatherer group trying to control entry into a 400-square-mile territory with a perimeter of 70 miles), more open access and some system of cooperative or reciprocal use rights are more likely to occur. Territories of hunter-gatherers are certainly not rigid, because of the needs mentioned previously to adjust group size to resources, level out demographic variance, and resolve conflict by fission. But in many cases, such as that of Australian aborigines, the regular association of local groups with particular areas is more or less constant. Peterson (1975) points out that an alternative strategy to prohibition of trespass and automatic defense of boundaries is the symbolic acceptance of outsiders as members of local groups before they make use of resources. If visitors announce their presence by making a fire, for example, a greeting ceremony involving exchange of fire or even hostile displays may take place, and the visitors may then be admitted to the resident camp. A local group may maintain an ideology associating a totemic clan with a particular tract of land and require ceremonial recognition of this special relationship. The ideology need not be reflected in the actual composition of the groups or the basis on which people explain their presence in a band.

Territoriality is not a constant, and its expression may change along with resource availability or degree of competition (Dyson-Hudson and Smith, 1978, p. 23). Exclusive as opposed to shared use of water holes may differ even among neighboring groups of San in different environments (Barnard, 1979). Some misconceptions about the size and territorial basis of hunter-gatherer groups have resulted from accepting as characteristic the structure of the band at one time of year or under specific historical circumstances (Speck and Eiseley, 1939; Hallowell, 1949; Leacock, 1954). When data for longer periods of time can be examined, such as those from several centuries of Hudson's Bay Company posts in the Canadian north analyzed by Knight (1965) and Bishop (1970), a much more satisfactory picture of ecological adaptation emerges. In the area between Hudson Bay and Lake Superior where population density was highest (one to twenty-five persons per forty square miles), game for food and furs was more difficult to secure. By 1810 the suppy of beaver as well as moose and other large animals was depleted by overhunting (Bishop, 1978, p. 213). Winter bands were therefore seldom larger than extended families, and they dispersed as widely as possible to maximize their hunting success. In this area family hunting territories were well defined and sanctions were enforced against trespass. Those Ojibwa groups with less population pressure (one person per eighty-five square miles) hunted large game, such as moose and caribou, and formed winter camps of twenty-five to thirty individuals. Mobile and relatively unpredictable game resources like moose tend to be incompatible with fixed exploitative zones, and the cooperation of six or seven men increases hunting efficiency (Bishop, 1978, p. 222). The bands moved over large areas and had no demarcated territories. Bishop (1972) showed that as the big game declined in the Ojibwa area and as furs became scarcer, the Indians were forced to rely on small nonmigratory animals such as rabbits. This meant camping in certain areas where rabbit snares could be visited daily. Large mobile winter groups could not be supported, and the resulting smaller family units depended more on trade goods. Under these circumstances, hunting territories were formed and defended. In those parts of Ontario to which moose began to return around 1900, a distinct lessening of territoriality took place (Bishop, 1970). Thus the size of the hunting group is correlated positively with the presence of large game animals and negatively with population density. Population pressure and the requirement for trade goods increase competition for resources and lead to the demarcation of hunting territories. The provision of food by trading posts also contributes to the increase in population density by preventing starvation. The systematic interdependence of population density, type of game available, hunting technique, and reliance on trade goods on the one hand with group size, frequency of movement, and territoriality on the other provides an elegant illustration of the ecological approach at work.

Chapter 3

NORTHWEST COAST FISHERMEN

The Northwest Pacific Coast of North America is the source of a rich, varied ethnographic lode that has been mined successfully and successively by three generations of American anthropologists. The Indian maritime hunters from Oregon to Alaska have provided a wealth of detailed cultural material, aesthetically exciting artifacts, and distinctive institutional complexes (such as the potlatch) that continue to challenge explanation. The Northwest Coast is a particularly stimulating arena for developing and testing anthropological theory because the various investigators hold in common a substantial body of data which is subject to alternative and sometimes conflicting interpretations. Because the traditional societies of the Northwest Coast have been altered so radically by white contact, historical and archaeological information about them is especially relevant in these cases. Over the last seventy years, some of the most creative American anthropologists have done fieldwork on the Northwest Coast and analyzed their findings from an ideological, social structural, or ecological point of view. All of these approaches are valid and potentially fruitful; moreover, they highlight some of the strengths and weaknesses of ecological analysis.

THE NATURE OF THE ENVIRONMENT

A fundamental issue has been the nature of the Northwest Coast physical environment. No one would disagree with the biologists' general characterization of this area as a Rainy Western Hemlock Forest Biome, with annual rainfall averaging more than 130 inches and associated with hemlock, wapiti, deer, red cedar, and Sitka spruce (Shelford, 1963, p. 211). But this description ignores the primary subsistence resources: fish supplemented by edible mollusks and marine game animals (Drucker, 1963). As Steward pointed out (1955, p. 39; see also Geertz, 1963, p. 6), the description of the total environment must be broken down to factors that are demonstrably relevant to the people who inhabit the area. Only by knowing the subsistence techniques, the means of shelter and bodily protection, and the transportation and communication devices of a particular human society can we determine what constitutes its "effective environment" (Netting, 1965). In the Northwest Coast, the combination of the Japanese Current and the Coast Range produces a moderate climate with heavy rains on the western slopes, feeding innumerable streams flowing to the sea (Drucker, 1963). The breeding habits of the salmon and certain other fish lead them to enter and ascend these streams to spawn in great numbers at certain seasons of the year. This chain of linked environmental variables became significant to the Indians only to the extent that they possessed tools and methods for catching the fish (traps, nets, harpoons, hooks, herring rakes, etc.) and preserving (by smoking, drying, or oil extraction) the large catches that could not be consumed during the short season. Other factors—such as the rugged and rocky terrain just inland from the coast—were negatively effective, inhibiting land hunting, agriculture, and overland travel, thus focusing attention on communication by water, which was in turn made possible by the cultural skills of boat building and coastal navigation (Drucker, 1963, p. 6). Craft work and manufacture were circumscribed by the presence of workable wood and the absence of similarly useful stone.

Many students of the Northwest Coast seem to have taken these environmental possibilities and hindrances for granted. The great annual salmon harvest was seen as providing an abundance of food and considerable periods of leisure within which the real business of cultural development—ceremonial, artistic, social, and political elaboration—

could go on. "Their civilization was built on an ample supply of goods, inexhaustible and obtained without excessive expenditure of labor" (Benedict, 1946, p. 156). Although the earlier anthropologists collected and described material culture and subsistence pursuits, they did not treat production, consumption, or labor expenditure quantitatively; nor did they have the opportunity to view these processes in time perspective, going back to a period when the cash economy had been less important. The mundane facts of subsistence were not only less attractive to ethnographers than were myths, feasts, and rituals, but they were also less amenable to collection by single observations or texts supplied by individual informants. Anthropologists themselves have often displayed a cultural bias favoring the verbal, aesthetic, and intellectual productions that characterize "high civilization" and that are the subject of scholarship in the liberal arts tradition. The relation of food getting, population dynamics, work organization, and settlement pattern to these factors was considered as uncomplicated as it was uninteresting.

More recently, several scholars have sought to expose the highly complex and systematic relations to environment that lie behind the sedentary villages, social ranking, artistic achievements, and dramatic, extensive ceremonialism that distinguish the Northwest Coast fishermen from most other hunting and gathering peoples. Wayne Suttles (1962), in particular, has sought to correct the idea that the Northwest Coast is a single ecological area with a consistent, dependable food supply everywhere. There is a wide variety of plant and animal resources, including twenty species of fish, ten different kinds of shellfish, forty species of waterfowl and shore birds, six land mammals, and three sea mammals as well as sprouts, bulbs, roots, and berries. Not all of these occur in any one area: blackberries and deer, for instance, thrive in burned-over country; shellfish vary according to whether their bed is gravel beach or sandspit; and the sockeye salmon follows regular migration routes along which it can be taken at only a few spots by reef nets (Suttles, 1962). Along with variations by location, these food sources vary in abundance from season to season and may show significant fluctuations from year to year. Contemporary records from canning factories show large-scale year-to-year differences in the abundance of pink salmon, traceable perhaps to

... variable water levels and temperatures in the spawning streams, variations in the permeability of the stream beds, occasional extreme floods, variable temperatures and salinity in the ocean . . . and the action of tides, currents, winds, and deep-water upwelling in the estuarine and inshore waters that are the habitat of the young salmon for weeks or perhaps months before they reach the open seas" (Piddocke, 1965).

It has been argued that cyclic alterations in the salmon run are not characteristic of areas outside that of the Coast Salish (with which Suttles is most directly familiar), and that farther north on the coast shellfish are not sparse and sporadic (Drucker and Heizer, 1967, p. 137). It seems probable, however, that the availability of plant foods and the populations of animals would vary spatially and seasonally as well as over longer time periods, and that these factors would strongly influence the local food quest. The severity of such fluctuations would also increase as growing human population density put greater pressure on local resources. Such questions cannot be settled except by painstaking collection of zoological and botanical data and reconstruction of subsistence patterns and the size and location of Indian settlements from historical and archaeological information. In the absence of direct quantitative evidence, conclusions on Northwest Coast subsistence must remain inferential (Suttles, 1968).

THE POTLATCH

We may at least hypothesize that the Northwest Coast environment was rich but that its resources were available differentially at various times, places, and years. This defines an ecological problem for any society residing in such a habitat: how best to control the resources in one's area, secure those that occur elsewhere, and cope with periodic scarcity. Anthropologists have been particularly concerned about whether certain social institutions found among such groups as the Coast Salish, Kwakiutl, Nootka, Haida, Tsimshian, and Tlingit could be seen as devices for adjusting to this environmental situation, or whether their functional explanations should be sought elsewhere. To some degree, this debate has crystallized in a series of models advanced for understanding the potlatch. There is general agreement on the definition of potlatch. Put simply, potlatching is "the giving away of food and wealth in return for recognition of the giver's social status" (Adams, 1973, p. 1). "In its formal aspects the potlatch is a congregation of people ceremoniously and often individually invited to witness a demonstration of family prerogative. Normally, the entire kin or local group acts as host to the visitors" (Barnett, 1938). Often the potlatch was an "ostentatious and dramatic distribution of property by the holder of a fixed, ranked and named social position to other position holders" (Codere, 1950, p. 63). It took place on numerous social occasions, including marriage, giving of a new name to a youth, assertion of a new rank by one who had inherited it, claim to a family crest and other privileges, raising of a new house, or introduction of a kin group chief. The festivities included a recitation of the host group's territorial rights and ceremonial privileges.

An early ethnographic approach to the potlatch appears in the work of Boas and his students. By 1886, Boas had turned away from an ecological perspective and sought on the Northwest Coast "a people among whom historical facts are of greater influence than the surroundings" (Stocking, 1968, p. 153). Historical reconstruction was itself impossible without the collection of a great deal of particular, accurate ethnographic detail before it had been obliterated by rapid cultural change. Boas, who witnessed Kwakiutl potlatches in the 1890s, was more interested in accurate description of the institution than analysis of it. In attempting to replace the evolutionary schemes and historical speculations of earlier anthropologists with scientific objectivity, he meticulously transcribed texts dealing with potlatch organization and etiquette based on actual occasions. Boas' emphasis was on Indian culture as the Indians themselves saw it, and he wanted to find out what people believed they themselves were doing (Drucker and Heizer, 1967, p. 2). The interpretations of the ethnographer were suspect. The orientation was what I have called ideological, tracing cultural facts to the minds of the culture bearers. Ruth Benedict's later (1946) use of Boas' material merely expanded the concept of mind from rational intelligence to total psyche. For her, the potlatch expressed the personality configuration that typified Kwakiutl culture. Titles, wealth, crests, and prerogatives were used in the potlatch in a contest to shame a rival and thus raise one's own relative glory. She emphasizes the destruction of coppers and food, the arrogance of chiefs, and their speeches expressing a "will to superiority" and "unabashed megalomania" (Benedict, 1946, p. 169). This indeed represents a possible, if somewhat melodramatic, reading of the potlatch texts (for a more balanced rendering of Kwakiutl personality, see Codere, 1956). But it may be misleading or at least incomplete to accept a people's own account of their actions as a full explanation of what is going on. We cannot expect the Kwakiutl or any social group to fully understand the meaning and relationships of their own institutions and to analyze their latent as well as manifest functions.

A second generation of anthropologists enlarged our view of the potlatch by stressing its key role in maintaining and articulating the social structure; to them it was something more than either cultural performance or psychodrama. It has been regarded as "a formal procedure for social integration, its prime purpose being to identify publicly the membership of a group and to define the social status of this membership" (Drucker and Heizer, 1967, p. 8). Potlatching confirmed or validated hereditary social status, but did not create it. The rivalry potlatch was a "process at civil law" which allowed personal and intergroup competition without physical violence (Drucker and Heizer, 1967, p. 133). The Kwakiutl potlatch was conducted between kin groups which also exchanged women and expressed the combination of hostility and solidarity characterizing the relationship of affines (Rosman and Rubel, 1971). These structural and functional views of the potlatch were considerably deepened by historical study, which indicated the responsiveness of the institution to rapidly changing socioeconomic circumstances. Codere (1950) showed that an increase in the size and frequency of potlatches after 1875 was correlated with (1) a precipitous decline in population, associated mainly with the introduction of imported diseases and leading to a surplus of graded potlatch positions with competing hereditary claims; (2) a great inflow of wealth from wage labor and trade with whites; and (3) a shift from warfare, which had been prohibited by white administrators, to the ceremonial "fighting with property" of the potlatch. Though based on a conception of the social importance of the potlatch as supporting an inclusive system of ranked statuses, this analysis of change in the potlatch could also be called ecological. It focuses on cultural contact as altering the demographic balance, economic equilibrium, and political controls of the Northwest Coast. Certainly the Kwakiutl and their neighbors were subject to a profound change in

their "intercultural environment" (Sahlins, 1964) or "regional population system" (Rappaport, 1967, 1969), and this change was sensitively
reflected in the potlatch.

   An ecological approach to the potlatch draws on the texts and early
descriptions, incorporates the history of change, and accepts the crucial
importance of the institution to social organization. But it goes on to
ask why such elaborate ranking should be adaptive, what purpose was
served by exchanges of wealth, and why competition should have such
high cultural value. Suttles (1962) views the potlatch as one of a series
of devices for reallocating resources to meet local and/or temporary
scarcity of subsistence goods resulting from environmental variations.
As he describes it for the Coast Salish, the process went something like
this. A kin or local group with a surplus of some food item, such as
fish or berries, could normally take this to its affinal relatives and get
wealth in the form of blankets or other durable goods in exchange; this
flow might later be reversed. If, however, one group produced a more
consistent surplus, wealth would tend to concentrate in its hands. Such
accumulation would be controlled by the potlatch, in which wealth was
converted into high status by one group and at the same time returned
to other communities, allowing them to continue the process. Similarly
it has been pointed out that the Kwakiutl could buy and sell food in
exchange for wealth objects, such as blankets, slaves, and canoes, and
these non-ceremonial transactions took place both when a group had a
serious food scarcity and when a wealthy group needed valuable goods
or food to use in a potlatch (Piddocke, 1965). At the potlatch distribution
of wealth, the host chief and his group acquired prestige in proportion
to their generosity, and if the gifts were not matched by the guests at
later potlatches, the relative prestige rankings of the leaders and their
groups could change (Piddocke, 1965). Even day-to-day gifts of food
within a Tlingit community were reinforced by prestige considerations,
and the wealthy were expected to give more for a service of equal value
than did lesser ranking persons.

> During a food shortage, those lucky enough to have a supply always distribute it
> among the villagers. For this they are publicly rewarded at some future potlatch
> and their renown is kept alive through songs and stories (Oberg, 1973, p. 97).

Even if groups were forced to obtain food by selling part of their wealth
during a famine, such scarcities were probably too infrequent to account

for the potlatch. In most instances of reciprocal potlatching, the participants probably broke even in material terms (Adams, 1981, p. 374). What was actually being redistributed in most instances was the chief's prestige (Adams, 1973, p. 89). The system could continue to operate because prestige is an immaterial, infinitely expandable commodity for which there is an unlimited demand.

Neat as this patterned exchange appears, questions have been raised as to whether formalized food-for-wealth giving actually took place and whether the recipients of food were really in need (Drucker and Heizer, 1967, p. 142). Giving food or wealth to the genuinely indigent, who had no ability to reciprocate, involved both parties in a *loss* of status. When need has been objectively present in recent times, as during the Great Depression, there is no record of the potlatch being used to sustain less fortunate groups (Adams, 1973: 92-93). It would seem, however, that the meals that accompanied potlatching and the parallel pattern of reciprocal feasts would stimulate individuals and groups to produce continuously at a level above their subsistence needs. There was no point at which further expenditure of effort in production of more of the same items was felt to be superfluous (Codere, 1950, p. 18). This stored surplus could provide a margin of safety for its owners, who could always decide to consume it rather than host a potlatch. Efforts to gather extra food supplies or to manufacture wealth goods would also tend to intensify the use of local resources and restricted niches. To the extent that each group used its immediate surroundings more effectively, the total carrying capacity of the area would be increased. The long-term security of any population is based not on its average production and consumption level but on the way it is able to weather periods of scarcity. If surplus production for potlatches or other types of interchange afforded such insurance, it would have given a selective advantage to the groups practicing it. In other words, socially rewarding occasions of exchange such as the potlatch provided an important social incentive to do what was ecologically beneficial—to build a surplus of food and gather wealth that could be exchanged for food.

COMPETITION AND THE CONTROL OF RESOURCES

The aggressive language and hostile gestures that accompanied much potlatch giving seem to reflect intense competition between local groups.

Was this competition merely a cultural happenstance maintained by the replication of a certain personality structure in each generation, or did it have roots in a struggle to control scarce resources? Since we have little trustworthy information on the relation between population and resources on the Northwest Coast in the aboriginal period, controversy continues over whether the Kwakiutl were sometimes close to the margin of survival (Piddocke, 1965) or whether any threat of starvation is "absurd" (Drucker and Heizer, 1967, p. 139). Practices of ownership and accounts of warfare, however, suggest that both individuals and groups were trying to ensure exclusive possession of dependable food sources and, when these proved insufficient, to wrest new territories from their neighbors (Ralston, n.d.). If the population could be supported with relative ease, and if, in addition, supplies of game and vegetable foods were unpredictable, as with many hunter-gatherer groups, we would expect fewer conflicts and much less clearly defined rights of tenure.

The relevance of ecological data on localized resources to potlatch behavior has been forcefully demonstrated in a study of the Southern Kwakiutl (Donald and Mitchell, 1975). In this area, good information exists on sixteen named local political groups, each consisting of a set of households sharing a winter village, exploiting the resources of a reasonably well-defined territory, and acting as a unit with its own chief in potlatch and military affairs. Salmon were taken on, or at the mouths of, streams within the territory (Fig. 3). Canadian Department of Fisheries estimates of salmon returning to spawn in each stream give some measure of the relative amount of salmon available in the past to each local group. Annual variation in number of fish per territory was also calculated, indicating returns of from 35 percent to more than 200 percent above and below the median (Donald and Mitchell, 1975, p. 332). Since the local groups were reliably ranked in prestige, their order of precedence can be correlated statistically with population size in the 1830s, which can in turn be predicted by median salmon run. The authors suggest that local groups with richer resource bases could support larger populations. A larger winter village would increase both available labor power—especially the number of women to butcher and preserve salmon—and the offensive and defensive advantages of the group in warfare. Though the correlation of local group rank with population and

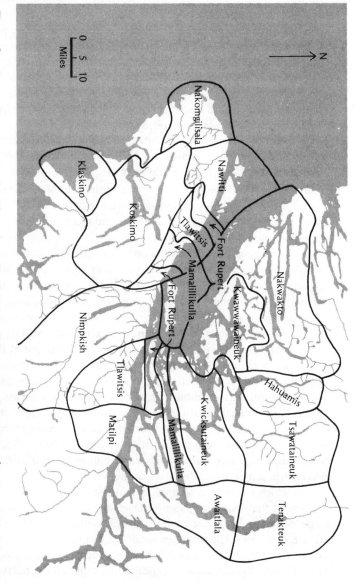

Figure 3. *Approximate territories of southern Kwakiutl local groups in the 1830s. (Redrawn from Leland Donald and Donald H. Mitchell, "Some Correlates of Local Group Rank among the Southern Kwakiutl,"* Ethnology *14: 325-346, 1975.)*

average salmon run size does not necessarily prove causation, it appears reasonable that "a larger population enables a local group to muster more goods and more people and thus achieve and maintain a relatively high local group rank" (Donald and Mitchell, 1975, p. 343). These findings emphasize the role of population in the Kwakiutl ecosystem and tend to support the ecological interpretation of Suttles as opposed to the sociological view that no important connections existed between resources and the potlatch.

Because of their fixed location, limited size, and relatively dependable production, sites for food getting were held and inherited by well-defined residential and kinship groups.

> The economic possessions of a Northwest Coast society were chiefly in the custody of, or nominally "owned" by, a line of eldest sons of eldest sons (or the matrilineal counterpart of such a line). By virtue of their stewardship these men were elevated to prominence. Directing the utilization of the natural resources as they did, they were the acknowledged heads of the groups—the heads of extended families. (Drucker, 1939, p. 60)

The rights to use an especially advantageous salmon fishing spot or a tract with a good annual harvest of berries were obviously valuable. Both the technical skills and the magical charms and rituals that accompanied and validated their use were also owned, as in the case of Nootka whaling methods (Drucker and Heizer, 1967, p. 142). Though communities may have moved seasonally to several areas with differing resources, they were firmly identified with the localities they used. Boundaries were defined and access rights were rigidly restricted, allowing sedentary settlements of up to 400 people and construction of substantial houses full of weighty possessions at main village sites on the coast. Intergroup feasting, which was probably more prevalent that potlatching in aboriginal times (Drucker and Heizer, 1967, p. 35) and which was also tied to the system of rank protocol, served to reaffirm these rights. "When the food had come from hereditarily owned tracts . . . , that fact and the genealogical route of transmission to the current possessors were announced" (Drucker and Heizer, 1967, p. 141). In pre-literate societies without central governmental control, a statement of claim to valuable resources could thus be publicly witnessed by those near neighbors who might be most likely to dispute it. Eating food with or receiving presents from a host group who recounted their ancestral claims to productive property and ceremonially passed it to its rightful heir was equivalent to accepting those claims and formally agreeing to respect them.

Nowadays among the Gitksan, living 200 miles inland along the Skeena River in British Columbia, fishing spots are not in short supply but traplines with their associated timber and mineral rights are sources of contention. Traplines are registered either to individual owners or to "companies," most of which consist of people from the same House (a grouping of three-generation matrilineal lineages). When a man inherits the name of a dead kinsman he also inherits the associated share of the trapline. "The cost of the potlatch at which the heir 'takes the name' is frequently recorded as 'paying for the trapline' . . ." (Adams, 1973, p. 12). Feasting to maintain these valuable rights is both a means to further land claims against the government and "a touchstone of Indian identity in a world increasingly dominated by the Whiteman's values" (Adams, 1973, p. 12).

The factor of prestige and relative social ranking, continually emphasized in Indian accounts and so fascinating to outside observers (perhaps because they come from class societies in which status, based partly on conspicuous consumption, is a much more absorbing topic than routine subsistence), may also have some foundation in the management of resources. The estate or property of a corporate kin group was often held in the name of its lineage chief, who functioned as a kind of executor. Leadership was more rigidly determined by descent among the Haida, Tsimshian, and Tlingit, whose resources were more concentrated (Suttles, 1962). The leader's superior status gave him the right to decide on moves from the winter village to the fishing station, and he often directed communal work on fish weirs or other large tasks (Drucker, 1963). Work of this kind, requiring intensive effort, cooperation, and scheduling, undoubtedly profited from some degree of central coordination and executive responsibility. Especially when the work force was divided to exploit spatially distant subsistence opportunities and its production was then pooled, it was probably more efficient to have jobs assigned and consumption regulated by someone who understood the entire operation. Social differentiation may have been further stimulated by periods of adversity.

> In Kwakiutl society . . . temporary and local food shortages could tend to establish an "economic chief," that is, the leader of a group not suffering from the current shortage. . . . The group's chief would be given the power to call

in some of the surplus catch of each fishing party in the village and redistribute this food in times of shortage. . . . Along with these real powers for action, the chief would acquire a social power, status, because of his importance to the community. (Weinberg, 1965)

Prestige—symbolized by titles, crests, the possession of important ceremonies, and potlatching—surrounded with meaning and power the individual who led the group, legitimizing his position and encouraging his followers to respond voluntarily to his direction. Thus honor was not an independent, culturally defined goal but the reward of good planning, well-administered cooperation, and the resulting group success in utilizing the environment.

Territorial rights and leadership based on status, as dramatically exemplified in the potlatch proceedings, were evidently not always adequate as means of preventing conflict over resources. Trespassing on hunting grounds, rivers, or berry-picking spots brought the risk of immediate fighting with the owning kin group (Boas, 1921, pp. 1345-1348). When it took place, warfare was ruthless and bloody. The object was to ambush or surprise an outnumbered group of the enemy and wipe it out. Tlingit warriors wearing wooden armor, helmets, and protective masks would attack at dawn, burning houses and plundering everything in their search for caches of valuables. Women and children were taken as slaves, while men were killed and scalped or beheaded (de Laguna, 1972, pp. 583-584). Though raids were traditionally ascribed to feelings of grief or shame, the desire to retaliate, or efforts to acquire the prestige associated with being utterly terrifying (Codere, 1950), an economic motivation also seems to have been present. One Kwakiutl group warred against a neighboring people until they were exterminated, then took possession of their territory (Drucker and Heizer, 1967, p. 19). Such conquest involved not only the appropriation of land, material wealth, and slaves, but also the capture of ceremonial prerogatives, which in effect gave title to these possessions. Warfare involving high casualties and territorial acquisition is rather infrequent in stateless societies and certainly rare among hunter-gatherers. It indicates that in certain localized instances, demographic pressures must have become quite severe. Though little real fighting occurred after 1837 because of government pacification (and perhaps also the sharp decrease in population), the rivalry potlatch provided a substitute (Codere, 1950).

The preparations and strategy were modeled on those of war, speeches were given to build up patriotic fervor, and the rhetoric was of violence.

One reason that the various explanations of the potlatch are not mutually exclusive is that the institution was obviously multifunctional (Piddocke, 1965, p. 258).* It had high diversion value, allowed emotional catharsis, validated ranked social statuses in such a way as to prevent conflict and contribute to social integration, and dramatized cultural values. But it also stimulated surplus production, allocated scarce goods in the absence of a market, encouraged social cooperation in production under the management of defined leaders, emphasized continuity of rights in resources, and channeled competition away from armed conflict. The potlatch adapted to changes in population, wealth, and political autonomy arising from culture contact. We know that the emphasis on these functions differed in various areas and in successive historical periods. It would also seem that an interpretation without ecological considerations would not do justice to the complexity and pivotal importance of the institution.

---

* For discussion of some of the problems encountered in functional analysis of the potlatch, see Orans (1975) and Adams (1981).

Chapter 4

EAST AFRICAN PASTORALISTS

THE CATTLE COMPLEX

On a map showing major regional cultural differences in Africa, a single tract stretches from southern Sudan through Kenya, Uganda, Rwanda, Burundi, Tanzania, Mozambique, and into parts of South Africa (Herskovits, 1924). This was christened the "East African Cattle Area" by Melville Herskovits, one of the first American anthropologists to work extensively with African materials (1926). The designation does not mean that this is the only part of Africa in which cattle are an important part of the economy or nomadic pastoralism exists. Herding is significant in a much larger area, especially in the vast savannahs bordering the Sahara on the south; this dispersion is graphically illustrated by a more recent map of cattle distribution in Africa (Deshler, 1963). Herskovits not only recognized this (1926, p. 248), but was also aware that many groups of agricultural peoples shared the area with the cattle keepers. The pastoralists themselves often depended more on grain products than on milk, meat, and blood for their support.* The distinctive traits of the East African Cattle Area mainly concerned the nonutilitarian purpose to which the animals were put and the peculiar attitudes their owners

---

*For a comparative typology of pastoralists, see Jacobs (1965).

held toward them. The "cattle complex" was an expression of dominant cultural *values* rather than ecological adaption. Stock raising in East Africa was considered technologically inefficient and economically irrational in comparison to its Euro-American counterpart, but its practices seemed to make sense in light of certain overarching values shared by the herders of this area. In delineating a cattle complex, Herskovits merely used a set of striking, often repeated facts from the literature to characterize a zone of common culture. A shared ideology or a cluster of psychological elements (Herskovits, 1926, p. 241) provided this unity and also furthered the approach of cultural relativity, which Herskovits shared with his contemporaries. By definition, one value position was as meaningful and worthy of study as another, and cultural integration could be shown without making invidious comparisons between the West and its primitive contemporaries.

Typical peoples of the East African Cattle Area were said to share the following traits:

1. Cattle are wealth used for social purposes rather than purely economic ones. Cows are "esteemed for the prestige and social status their possession brings" and are thus valuables comparable to Trobriand kula items or Northwest Coast coppers (Herskovits, 1965, p. 240). But they are not equivalent to money, because nothing can be acquired for them but wives (Herskovits, 1965, p. 264). Even the transfer of cows as bridewealth is regarded by those who practice it as a noneconomic institution: "Its aim is to legitimize a mating and to permit a man to lay proper claim to his children. . ." (Herskovits, 1965, p. 175).

2. Cattle are used only in a limited way as a food source. The subsistence economy of most herding groups is based on farming. Cattle supply only milk and are not used as beasts of burden. They are eaten only on certain ceremonial occasions or when they die. The people are reluctant to part with cattle and do not wish to kill them. The inference here is that meat is rarely consumed because the live animals constitute wealth.

3. At the root of the cattle complex is a strong personal attachment to the beasts, manifested in affection for and identification with individual animals. This emotional closeness leads to

their association with such rituals as the ceremonies at birth, death, marriage, and initiation.

These characteristics doubtless reflect what people say and think about their cows. But do they also mirror the way in which the animals are actually used and the ecological rationale for such practices? Can we be content to say that the obvious love of many Africans for their cattle is based on nothing stronger than mutual attraction?

THE HERDING HABITAT

Fortunately, we have an impressive series of recent studies by Evans-Pritchard, Gulliver, Schneider, Deshler, Dyson-Hudson, Goldschmidt, and others. They consider in detail the facts of pastoral life in well-defined environmental contexts. These reports also compare the economic advantages of herding to alternative types of subsistence in the same habitat and analyze the adaptive function of specific social institutions. In general, they support the contentions that "the social attitudes toward cattle are related to and may have arisen from subsistence or survival imperatives" (Deshler, 1965).

We must ask first whether pastoralists' devotion to cattle keeping results from the cultural value placed on livestock or whether it is the most effective means at their disposal for utilizing certain biomes. Most of the nomadic herding peoples inhabit a plateau of ancient rock faulted by the Great Rift Valley and pierced by volcanic mountains. The surface slopes from 6000 to 2000 feet in elevation and varies in its plant cover from tropical savannah with acacia and thorn forest to semi-desert. Grass may grow 3 to 5 feet high in portions of the area, but it is usually shorter, often occurring in dry tussocks. Water is the major environmental limitation. Precipitation is often no more than 20 to 30 inches annually, and it is extremely irregular. Rainfall increases with altitude. Areas wet enough to support forest may also harbor the tsetse fly, which infects cattle with the deadly trypanosomiasis. The parts of East Africa where herding is dominant are generally those in which water is scarce and rain unpredictable, and thus where agriculture is at its least productive and dependable. Because the mobility of herd animals allows the herders to evade the climatic vicissitudes that would result in crop failure, pastoralism is a recurrent adaptation to steppes, deserts, and dry savannahs. In an environment in which vegetable food is insufficient for nourishing humans directly but is capable of supporting grazing animals, "the adoption of a pastoral economy constitutes an advance in man's capacity to exploit the area" (Aschmann, 1965).

The question remains regarding the extent to which local populations correctly evaluate the environmental potential and make decisions that maximize their subsistence opportunities. Evans-Pritchard's pioneering work (1940) on the Nuer elegantly outlines an ecosystem in which the rhythm and nature of subsistence activities are conditioned largely by the physical environment. The flatness of Nuerland in the southern Sudan, its heavy clay soils, and the annual flooding of the Nile and its tributaries necessitate a clustering of population on elevated sandy ridges during part of the year. Land for planting the staple (sorghum) is therefore limited; the crop is further menaced by violent rainstorms and depredations of elephants, birds, and insects. Drought comes too soon for a second sowing. With present climate and technology, no considerable increase in Nuer horticulture would be profitable. Cattle, even if they do not provide the bulk of subsistence, are thus an important insurance factor and are probably the most effective means of using the seasonally innundated plains of grass. According to Nuer values, herding is preferable to horticulture; this attitude is comparable to the hunter-gatherer's stress on game as opposed to collected vegetable foods. The herding of cattle necessitates seasonal movements, first to small, dispersed cattle camps where dairying and fishing are pursued, and later in the dry season to temporary settlements of several hundred people at permanent sources of water. The cycle of seasonal activities effectively determines both of these settlement patterns. Evans-Pritchard's account suggests that these same factors are influential in fostering the sociopolitical pattern of segmentary lineages, though he specifically disclaims such a connection (Evans-Pritchard, 1940, p. 284). A point-by-point comparison of environment in neighboring East African areas has been used by Gulliver (1955) to account for varying proportions of stock, herding practices, emphasis on agriculture, distance and variability of nomadic movements, family fission, and inheritance patterns between the Jie and Turkana peoples, who appear to have diverged from a single common tradition.

Study of several East African tribes, each with agricultural and pastoral sections, has made possible more precise isolation of some factors influencing relative dependence on crops or herds (Goldschmidt, 1965). In a generalized altitudinal profile of East Africa, the geographer Porter (1965) has shown the relation among rainfall, elevation, and crops, along with the zones inhabited by disease-bearing organisms (Fig. 4). This indicates that the lower altitudes, with greatly variable rainfall averaging between 10 and 20 inches annually, are unsuitable for any of the important food crops. They provide only the grasses and browse which will support grazing animals. Mapping rainfall probabilities and comparing this water supply over a number of years with water need (the transpiration requirement of incoming radiant energy) makes it possible to compute the proportion of years in which adequate rain for crop maturing is probably available. Where this probability was 0.9 (9 out of 10 years with adequate precipitation), a dense population of farmers could subsist. Intermediate areas with a probability of 0.3 had chronic crop failure and famine, and areas with a 0.1 average were largely pastoral, showing only desultory agriculture. This means of determining subsistence uncertainty by measuring the vagaries of climate is called "subsistence risk" (Porter, 1965). If alternative technologies are available, it is by no means certain that a human group will settle rapidly on the most advantageous one, but over time the tendency is clearly to select the subsistence adaptation that shows more frequent success and fewer occasions of failure. The high proportion of pastoralists in water-scarce areas and the proportion of effort devoted to agriculture appear closely correlated to the local pattern of subsistence risk. Anthropologists whose data are limited to one or two years of fieldwork among one tribe and who lack or ignore long-term records of environmental fluctuations cannot properly evaluate the utility of a particular subsistence strategy.

Though scarcity of rainfall, pasture, and reliable stock watering sites may appear to be harsh physical constraints, the pastoral environment also offers some distinct advantages. Ecological studies in the Sahel zone south of the Sahara in West Africa indicate that though the annual grasses have low biomass, their relatively high protein content provides good quality forage (Breman and de Wit, 1983). Cattle graze selectively, choosing the vegetation with better nutrition and digestibility, and

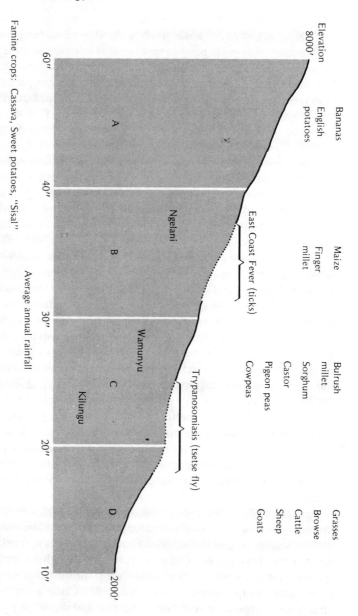

Figure 4. *Generalized altitudinal profile of East Africa showing relationships among rainfall, elevation, and crops. (From P. W. Porter, "Environmental Potentials and Economic Opportunities." Redrawn by permission of the American Anthropological Association from the American Anthropologist 67: 409–420, 1965.)*

Famine crops: Cassava, Sweet potatoes, "Sisal"

showing higher production than they do on the more abundant but
nitrogen-poor pastures of the savanna farther south. Transhumant annual
migrations of hundreds of kilometers allow herders to derive the benefits
of northern Sahel grazing in the short rainy season and survive the dry
months by retreating to permanent water supplies along rivers (Breman
and de Wit, 1983). Livestock productivity in terms of weight gain, calving
rate, and calf survival is better among migrating herders than among
sedentary farmers in the same savanna areas (Haaland, 1977).

This does not mean that cattle are kept only on marginal agricultural
lands. Herds are also maintained in agricultural areas of high human
population density, such as Rwanda and Burundi, where they "might
be regarded as a luxury because animal production yields fewer calories
per acre than crop production" (Deshler, 1963). It has been said that
even such classic pastoral peoples as the Masai could also practice hunting or farming, and that their choice of subsistence reflects attitudes
and religious beliefs rather than the environment (Jacobs, 1965). Where
latitude in mode of food production is possible, we must obviously consider such factors as local nutrition, population pressure on resources,
and the history of the group in order to understand the relative proportions of agriculture and stock raising practiced. But it would seem apparent that the highest development of the cattle complex should occur
in societies in which the animals make a major contribution to subsistence.

This is clearly documented in accounts of Karimojong, a herding
people of Uganda, by the Dyson-Hudsons (1969). The territory of this
tribe is remarkable for the unevenness and unpredictability of its rainfall. Over thirty-four years, one station registered amounts varying from
18 to 58 inches. Herding strategy must take into consideration not only
the presence of permanent water and the availability and nutritional
status of grass (when dry, perennial grasses are nutritionally deficient),
but also the necessity of avoiding sticky, wet clay soils where cows may
fall, tall grasses that may shelter predators, tick-borne East Coast fever,
and the presence of enemy raiders. For these reasons cattle may be
moved frequently over great distances. Though a Karimojong settlement
of 250 people may use less than one square mile for house sites and
gardens, its cattle may graze over 500 square miles in the course of two
years. Whereas crops are ruined by a drought of three to four months

during the growing season, the more mobile animals can simply follow the rainfall. The extent of nomadic movement varies among families, depending on the number of cows held, the amount of labor that can be mobilized, and the idiosyncrasies of the herd owner (R. Dyson-Hudson, 1972). Those who own fewer cows devote more effort to tending crops. The most reliable food resources remain, however, the milk, blood, and meat of livestock.

The Karimojong are a textbook illustration of cattle complex traits. To them cattle mean many things—wealth, a legacy to sons, formal contracts of friendship, validation of marriage, sacrifice, and a proper object of affection. A Karimojong boy "is given a specifically named male calf to identify himself with, to care for and to decorate, to commemorate in song at dances and beer parties, and to incorporate into the style of his most formal name as an adult." Important as these elements are, "they are cultural elaborations of one central fact: cattle are the major source of subsistence for the Karimojong. First, last and always the role of cattle in Karimojong life is to transform the energy stored in the grasses, herbs and shrubs of the tribal area into a form easily available to people" (R. and N. Dyson-Hudson, 1969).

ECONOMIZING WITH COWS

Though stock raising may be the optimal way to use dry environments marginal to agriculture, do herders make the best use of their animals? Or do they avoid killing cattle for meat when it would be economically advantageous to do so, and do they on the other hand slaughter wastefully at ceremonies? The Pakot of west central Kenya have sizeable amounts of livestock, averaging 10 to 20 head of cattle per adult male, plus 10.5 goats and 3.4 sheep (Schneider, 1957). Like other groups of the East African Cattle Area, they dislike killing their animals except in a ritual context. Steers are killed in a ceremonial manner, with the initiated men ranged in order of age-set precedence in a half circle. The meat is cut up in a prescribed fashion and not allowed to touch the ground. The feast is accompanied by a divination of entrails, an elaborate distribution of meat, and prayers led by elders. The eating of meat and milk on the same day is taboo. Cattle are sacrificed on ten specified occasions ranging from the conclusion of intertribal peace to the payment of an adulterer's fine. The ratio of adult cows to steers (about 4 or 5 to 1) reveals that animals are killed selectively. A cow is not killed because its milk and offspring make it the most valuable form of productive capital. Steers appear to be slaughtered when they reach their prime.

Cattle may be consumed merely to satisfy hunger, but the Pakot object to killing for family use only, because the meat is not shared. Even if some techniques of preservation are known, wide distribution of fresh meat is especially efficient under tropical conditions. Not only does it ensure that no spoilage takes place, but it also establishes numerous obligations to reciprocate within the community. Each Pakot man is expected to give at least one meat feast a year. Thus forty to fifty of these occasions may take place annually in a neighborhood. A sacrifice is the preferred reason for a feast, and the most frequent kind of feast given is one to request the prayers and goodwill of one's neighbors. For this feast there is no fixed time, and it is often requested by the local community. When cattle are scarce, ritual celebrations are correspondingly restricted. Among the neighboring Karimojong, steers are ceremonially slaughtered most frequently during periods of poor rainfall or crop failure. Thus meat may substitute to some extent for other foods in the human diet (R. and N. Dyson-Hudson, 1969). Ritual consumption would therefore appear to be a most effective way to utilize the meat of large animals fully in such a way as to promote community cooperation and solidarity.

Though Pakot men consider the hide colors and horns of their cattle aesthetically pleasing and sing songs about the beautiful special steer with which each man is identified, their values do not preclude the use of those particular animals in exchange. Cows have a higher economic value than even the prize steers. These steers may be used for food or trade despite the personal attachment (Schneider, 1957). Steers are traded for grain and their hides sold. They are also traded for cows, in a partnership with continuing clanlike relationships; this trading tends to spread the risk of capital loss through warfare and disease. Though cattle given as bridewealth legitimize a change in social relationships, they also have an economic return, both in the agricultural, craft, and household work of women and in the provision of new sons as herding assistants and daughters who will themselves be the source of more bridewealth. Cattle are thus not isolated in a separate economic sphere with its own rules, but are negotiable wealth in a wide variety of circumstances.

It is no accident that the English word "pecuniary" is derived from the Latin *pecus*, meaning "cattle," and ultimately from the Indo-European root *peku*, referring to cattle, movable property, and wealth. If the herd animals of East Africa serve as a medium of exchange and a store of value, there is every reason to call them money (Schneider, 1974). Harold Schneider regards the Turu of Tanzania as "economic men" relating scarce resources to multiple ends. Cows are certainly esteemed for the prestige their possession brings, as Herskovits would have it, but this does not mean that their owners are not economizing in rational and ultimately predictable ways. The Turu show a marked tendency to trade up, converting their grain surpluses into animals that yield more per input of labor than agricultural land and that reproduce themselves. Cattle in turn may be productively invested in bridewealth that increases the supply of available labor, grazing land to support more cows, and grain for making beer to sell on the market. Cattle held as wealth, loaned to poorer neighbors, or sacrificed to the ancestors may bring an indirect return to the individual through the obligation of neighbors to him and the deference shown on social occasions (Schneider, 1970, p. 88). Power and influence are the ultimate rewards. Livestock are sacrificed, "as is money in most economies, to social status. The Turu . . . is a maximizer not of goods but of status. Utility in its purest form is social, not material" (Schneider, 1974, p. 260).

THE ADVANTAGES OF LARGE HERDS

During the colonial period, governments made frequent efforts to limit the numbers of grazing stock or to cut the size of herds in order to prevent overgrazing and subsequent degradation of the environment. The cultural emphasis of the cattle keepers on large herds was said to show the primacy of the "prestige economy" over more rational considerations of long-term survival. There is no doubt that overgrazing occurs, that it reduces range carrying capacity (Deshler, 1963), and that pastoralists strongly resist herd reduction or systematic culling. The severity of the climate and the low productivity of African cattle may furnish some explanation for this insistence by every individual on having as many head of stock as possible. Among the Dodos or Dodoth of northeastern Uganda, some 75,000 cattle may be dependent on as few as eighteen water holes during the dry season (Deshler, 1965). Herd losses from malnutrition may in some years run as high as 10 to 15 percent, and the average weight loss for a 650-pound animal may be 60 to 100 pounds. Thus mortality is high among young stock, and even animals that live may require six to seven years to attain full growth. Samburu herders point out that a certain percentage of animals are likely to die in any prolonged dry spell. A man who loses one-third of his stock is much better off if he begins with sixty cows than with six (Spencer, 1965).

Only 20 percent of a Dodoth herd may be giving milk at any one time. Since each cow must also feed her own calf, only about one quart a day remains for human consumption in the wet season, and one-fourth to one-sixth of a quart in the dry (Plate 1). This means that milk production per cow is estimated at 300 to 400 pounds annually, compared to a U.S. average of 8000 to 12,000 pounds. At this rate the 20,000 Dodoth probably get an average of only one pint of milk each per day. Once a month during the wet season, blood is collected by piercing the cow's jugular vein with a small arrow. One or two pints are taken; it is consumed most frequently by young men in the nomadic cattle camps. With meat being eaten once a week or less, the total contribution of dairy products, blood, and flesh to the Dodoth diet is probably less than one-third of all calories (Deshler, 1965). The utility of cattle resides both in the importance of high-quality protein to the nutrition and in their value as famine insurance. With recurrent droughts cutting grain production and the opportunities for gathering wild foods, cattle provide a way to store subsistence reserves on the hoof. Among nomadic pastoral peoples "the keeping of large herds is closely linked to the need to protect the household against the effects of drought or epidemics as well as to food requirements during a particular dry period" (Dahl and Hjort, 1976, p. 17). Considering the threat of attrition to herds and alternative resources, along with the low productivity of cattle in a hostile environment, it is little wonder that the growth of the herd should be a universal positive value among all pastoralists (Aschmann, 1965).

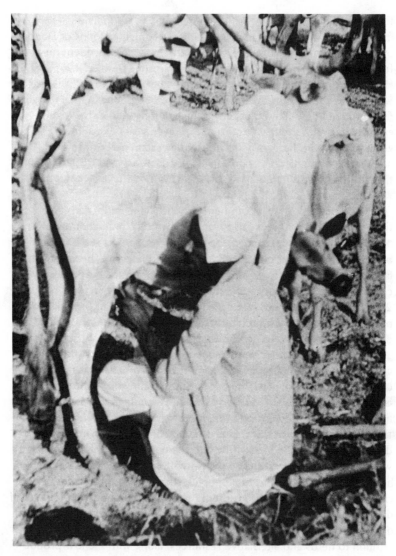

Plate 1. *A Fulani herder from northern Nigeria milks one of his long-horned, humped cows. Note that the animal is hobbled and the calf is tied to its front legs.*

The lack of conservation practices among East African herders may result from their historic tendency to migrate over large areas, leaving when the pasture was exhausted and fighting for control of new territories. It was not worthwhile to maintain good grazing, which might actually invite outside competition (R. and N. Dyson-Hudson, 1969). Since rights to the use of resources were common to all tribe members, whatever one man saved would merely benefit his neighbor. Finally, the periodic cattle and human epidemics reduced populations in spite of all efforts, and thus allowed the vegetation to recover (R. and N. Dyson-Hudson, 1969). The Karimojong thus clearly aim to preserve and enlarge their herds rather than to conserve their grazing land.

Karimojong cattle are if anything less productive than those of the Dodoth. Only 12 percent of their herds give milk, and some 40 percent or more are male stock. Unproductive animals and steers are not eliminated because market prices are too low to make this course of action worthwhile. If kept alive, this stock provides blood, bride-wealth, formal friendship gifts, and, eventually, meat. As the Dyson-Hudsons (1969) emphasize, the Karimojong are not attempting to maximize the number of animals while limiting the number of workers, as Western dairy or ranching enterprises do to produce large marketable surpluses. Rather, their goal is a regular daily supply of food for the largest number of people who can exist as relatively self-sufficient pastoralists. Their system is a rational solution to the problems of supporting a substantial population in a variable environment. To change it would require altering the ecological constraints, either by building more dams and wells and improving agricultural seed or by resettling some of the people. Technological development would require capital investment that is difficult for a developing economy to muster, whereas relocation of population would create serious political strains (R. and N. Dyson-Hudson, 1969).

Pastoral economies are by no means insulated from the demands of expanding market economies. With rising standards of living and urbanization in some parts of Africa have come higher prices for meat, especially beef and mutton. When herders increase their cattle and sheep, they put pressure on grasses and decrease the proportion of browsing animals like goats and camels. As the mixed herds that spread the risks of subsistence production decline, commercially oriented pastoral nomads may be more vulnerable to drought (Swift, 1977). Turkana nomads in one of the most arid parts of northwestern Kenya showed the value of having sizeable diversified herds of camels, small stock (sheep and goats), and cattle during a severe 1980-81 dry period. Though the herds were dispersed to meet differing requirements for pasture and water, there were losses of over 60 percent of small stock, 44 percent of camels, and 50 percent of cows (Wienpahl, 1984). Dry season starvation, animal predation, disease (some of which was induced in weakened animals by the return of the rains), and major raiding by Turkana bandits and Pokot were responsible for these losses, but the four households of Turkana under observation were able to survive on the milk, blood, and meat of the animals and some purchased maize meal. Though camels can endure drought better than other livestock, they reproduce slowly, and it was the goats and sheep that could replenish their numbers most rapidly when favorable precipitation conditions resumed (Wienpahl, 1984).

PASTORALIST PERSONALITY

Observers have always recognized that pastoralists show certain distinctive personality traits. Colonial administrators are often accused of preferring the independent, aggressive, culturally conservative herders to submissive, superstitious farmers who acculturate rapidly. Anthropologists are just beginning to investigate the links between subsistence types and character structure. What little information we have would suggest that personality traits do not adapt so quickly to ecological readjustments as do features of social organization. Indian tribes from farming backgrounds and tribes who had previously been hunter-gatherers took on similar band and tribal structures, despite the difference in their backgrounds, when they became mounted bison hunters on the plains. They continued, however, to have different child-training methods, sexual attitudes, and reactions to intragroup aggression (Gladwin, 1957). The question arises whether psychological factors on a group level have relatively little adaptive value or whether they merely show a kind of psychological lag, altering their form more slowly than other cultural elements. Herskovits (1926) felt that psychological traits were of central importance in defining the cattle complex, but he realized the difficulty of elucidating them.

A controlled comparison of attitudes and personality characteristics in four East African groups has been carried out (Edgerton, 1965). The Sebei and Pakot are Bantu speakers, while the Kamba and Hehe are Nilotes. On the basis of standard interviews, Rorschach tests, TAT-like pictures, and responses to color slides, it was possible to show that there were regular differences among tribes and between linguistic groups. Striking contrasts were also found between pastoral and agricultural sections of each tribe; these appeared to be a function of ecological orientation. Statistically significant differences were as follows:

1. Farmers value hard work; herders do not.

2. Farmers divine and consult one another; herders act individually.

3. Farmers are more suspicious and hostile to their fellows than are herders.

4. Farmers tend to be indirect, abstract, given to fantasy, more anxious, and less able to control their emotions and impulses. Herders are more direct, open, and bound to reality; their emotions, though more constricted, are under control.

5. The more pastoral the economy, the more that society will maximize and value independence of action in its male members (Edgerton, 1965).

Some of these traits relate clearly to the subsistence success of pastoralists. A man who must direct the movements of his herd and decide independently on an optimum strategy for using scarce resources must learn to make decisions and act on them (Goldschmidt, 1965). Since cattle are a volatile form of wealth, a man has the freedom to raise his own social status through initiative and skill. On the other hand, he must be willing to defend his animals aggressively from predators and military raids and to show fortitude and endurance when he meets with hardship (Plate 2). Attitudes of resignation and detachment are evident in the face of droughts and epidemics (Evans-Pritchard, 1940; see also Stenning, 1959). Self-containment, control, bravery, and a realistic appraisal of the world (Goldschmidt, 1965) are necessary responses to

Plate 2. *Fulani herdsmen take their cattle south for sale as meat in southern Nigerian cities. One man wears a short sword to defend his animals and carries a teakettle for ablutions before Moslem prayers.*

the individual dangers and opportunities of pastoralism in an uncon-
trolled, frequently hostile environment. As studies of personality and
culture return to favor in anthropology, they should consider and
define more precisely the place of personality in the system of mutually adapted ecological variables.

THE LINEAGE: A MODEL OF SOCIETY
IN THE MIND OR ON THE GROUND?

Some, though by no means all, pastoral groups in East Africa structure
their society and order their political life on the basis of the segmentary
lineage. The use of genealogical links from a named ancestor through
successively less inclusive groups of kin was brilliantly demonstrated by
Evans-Pritchard (1940) as forming the political framework of the Nuer.
Large groups called clans comprise all individuals who trace descent
through males to the common ancestor. The clan is subdivided into
maximal lineages which are further segmented into major, minor, and
minimal lineages—the last having a time depth of three to five generations from living persons. Marriage, ceremonial relations, hospitality,
and the peaceful or warlike settlement of disputes are regulated by
lineage membership and by the degree of relationship in genealogical
terms between groups. In simplified fashion, we can think of a minimal
lineage as consisting of the descendants of a single grandfather and
bearing his name. This group is cohesive in disputes when opposed to
men descended from the grandfather's brother but combines with
these same relatives against more distantly related patrilineal kin.
Territorial sections within a tribe are named for the clans and lineages
dominant within them. This system defines a series of articulated
groupings and provides a political organization in the absence of rulers
or chiefs.
 Paradoxically, the definitive framework of clan and lineage has little
apparent effect on the composition of local villages or cattle camps;
the ideology of descent does not determine residence. Given the vicissitudes of rainfall, pasture growth, and water sources in an arid environment, it is understandable that nomadic herding units should expand,
contract, and combine, both seasonally and at unpredictable times.
But these subsistence groups are often not made up of patrilineal kin

despite the rigid genealogical model which the people themselves use
to characterize their society (Spooner, 1973). Nuer wet season settlements include a large proportion of people related through women
(sister's children, mother's brother's offspring, wife's siblings, and so on)
or are entirely unrelated, such as captured Dinka (Evans-Pritchard,
1951). Affinal relatives and matrilocality appear more important in
many of the transactions of daily life than lineage mates in the same
community. Nuer change residence in search of land for cultivation,
water for cattle, or more congenial neighbors, frequently going to the
homes of married sisters. The lineage, on the other hand, remains dispersed, and the clan does not meet together or function as a corporate
group. Actual group membership and coresidence may indeed be based
economically on the cattle debts contracted by a man to his wife's kin.
Creditor and debtor, bound together for mutual advantage, may cooperate against a common foe (Glickman, 1971). Their lineages may in
time fuse as genealogical relationships are rearranged to suit the realities
of current cooperation. It is possible that patriliny is maintained as an
ideology (Glickman, 1971) or a kinship idiom (Spooner, 1973) referring to a widespread rather than a local social grouping. If resources
are unstable, territorial attachment may include far-flung grazing
grounds and water holes. A number of subsistence groups may claim
rights to this territory and defend it by appealing to the principle of
common descent (Spooner, 1973). Their claim is encoded in a patrilineal genealogy, ideally stable and fixed but in fact subject to covert
adjustments and occasional revision. The value of such a shared identity
lies in its potential for calling up allies for defense or mounting a
numerically superior attack on groups lacking the massing potential of
the segmentary lineage (Sahlins, 1961). The genealogical model also
provides a set of easily adopted social roles and statuses which mediate
and render predictable relationships with spatially separated groups in
the course of transhumance movements or migration. For regional
territorial and political dealings, the ideology of descent within a lineal
kin group appears useful, but it cannot be applied to such mundane
aspects of life as residence and economic cooperation without destroy-
ing their necessary flexibility.

Chapter 5

CULTIVATORS

One of the richest fields for applying the ecological approach to anthropology has been the study of agriculture and its relation to society. Here all the subdisciplines—archaeological, cultural, and physical anthropology—have rediscovered the stimulation of attacking common problems from several points of view. An understanding of the origins of agriculture and its prehistoric development not only throws light on contemporary changes in farming but is itself illuminated by investigations of nutrition, disease vectors, and mortality patterns.

Types of food production vary tremendously, and the complex interaction of climate, land, technology, population, settlement pattern, work group composition, food consumption, and rights to the means of production is little understood. When they considered these matters at all, anthropologists of former times did so in scattered and generally unconnected chapters on environment, material culture and farming techniques, kin groups, villages, and land tenure. Turn-of-the-century scholars were much more interested in rain dances than in rain, and their short (or nonexistent) periods of fieldwork allowed them to collect myths of a corn god but few facts on the seasonal cycle of corn growing. When longer spans of participant observation became the rule, the focus of interest was rather narrowly confined to social organization.

> The tendency in social anthropology has been to study societies as if they
> were isolated, self-sufficient systems, subsisting on thin air, with no visible
> roots in the soil. The guiding principle, derived in large part from Durkheim
> and more explicitly from Radcliffe-Brown, has been that social facts require
> sociological explanations. (Gray, 1964, p. 6)

Thus little attention was paid to families as units of resource exploitation and consumption; inheritance was handled legalistically; and settlement patterns were "taken for granted as basic, irreducible data which
are of scientific interest mainly as determinants of kinship systems or
'rules of residence' . . ." (Gray, 1964, p. 7). In order to place these
factors functionally in the wider perspective of techno-environmental
processes, it was first necessary to understand the nature of specific
agricultural systems.

SYSTEM AND KNOWLEDGE IN
NON-WESTERN AGRICULTURE

A seminal contribution of recent anthropologists, geographers, and
agronomists investigating "primitive" agriculture has been the revelation
of its systematic aspects, including profound practical knowledge of
weather, soils, plants, and pests. Westerners have long held a distinctly
ethnocentric model of agriculture. They knew it as mixed farming with
grain crops and domestic animals—a distinctive Old World pattern that
is dominant from Ireland to India (Arensberg, 1963). Here bread
grains were planted in pure stands once or twice a year; domestic
animals were maintained for milk, meat, and draft purposes; and fodder
was stored when natural forage was not obtainable. Fields were plowed
and used annually, with fertility maintained by manuring and crop
rotation. Farms and livestock were privately owned, and land and
labor entered the market.

Western observers found that in the tropics of America, Africa, and
Oceania food could be grown in quite different ways. Unfamiliar grain
crops such as maize, sorghum, rice, and millet replaced wheat and
barley. Root crops, including yams, taro, sweet potatoes, and manioc,
were often of primary importance. Domestic animals, on the other
hand, were rare and economically peripheral. Interpretations of these
factors varied, but they were almost universally assumed to be inferior.

Native farmers were considered ignorant and uninformed, their tools primitive, and their cultivation rudimentary. It was said that people could not work hard because the climate was debilitating, that they lacked the true religion of honest effort, or that they had such natural abundance (fruit always ripe for the picking) that they didn't need to exert themselves (Curtin, 1964). Their methods were judged wasteful of land and timber and irreparably damaging to natural fertility. Describing the apparent chaos of an African garden, de Schlippe (1956, p. 101) says of a Zande homestead: ". . . no fields can be seen. The thickets of plants surrounding the homestead seem as patchy and purposeless as any wild vegetation. It is impossible to distinguish a crop from a weed." Land was often communally held and used in what appeared to be random fashion. The predominant impression was one of disorder.

When the Western methods that worked so well in the temperate zone were applied to the tropics, however, the results were often disastrous. Fields were washed away, weeds choked the crops, and the animals died. Observations of indigenous agricultural systems supplied some proven methods for raising food under such fundamentally different environmental conditions. The key to these was an understanding of shifting cultivation, a type of agriculture in which impermanent fields are planted with crops for shorter periods of years than they are left fallow (Conklin, 1961). This system is also called swidden, slash-and-burn, and field-forest rotation, and local terms such as *caingin, ladang, citimene,* and *milpa* are frequent in the literature (Conklin, 1954).* Shifting cultivation (which does not necessarily imply shifting residence) was found to follow an orderly schedule, to incorporate extensive knowledge, and to utilize ecologically sound techniques.

Agricultural activities under shifting cultivation must be scheduled according to environmental variables, plant growth patterns, and labor availability. Once cut, trees and brush must have time to dry out in order to burn as completely as possible. The bed of ash is necessary for a good crop; in areas of heavy rainfall several partial burns may be necessary to achieve this. The Bemba of Zambia utilize their dry

---

*For extensive bibliographies on shifting cultivation, see Conklin (1961) and Gourou (1966, p. 41).

woodland habitat by pollarding the trees and burning their branches to form roughly circular gardens incorporating the ash (Richards, 1939). Crops must also be planted at planned intervals. Where crops do not store well (sweet potatoes in the New Guinea highlands, for example), new fields are opened at regular intervals to provide a continuous harvest. Often, land disturbed by the digging of a root crop or peanuts is replanted immediately. Shifting cultivators may follow a rotational system, such as the Zande practice of planting peanuts and maize in a new clearing, followed in the same year by eleusine (finger millet) with sorghum, sesame, melons, and other associated small crops. The eleusine association may be repeated in the following year, mixed with cassava, which will continue to grow after the grain and vegetables are harvested (de Schlippe, 1956, pp. 122ff.). Where land must be rested periodically, the farmer can gauge the degree of soil regeneration accurately by means of changes in the plant cover and soil consistency. Land use is determined not by chemical tests but by noticing the natural vegetation, which is "the best indicator available of the potential of any area of land" (Allan, 1965, p. 14). By reusing a field only when its fertility has been restored, the shifting cultivator can maintain the ecological equilibrium of his environment.

Shifting cultivators display a knowledge of soils, food plants, and cropping techniques that is amazingly wide, accurate, and practical. The Hanunóo, a mountain people of Mindoro in the Philippines, know ten basic and thirty derivative soil and mineral categories. They also understand the effects of erosion, exposure, and overfarming. Their repertoire of 1500 useful plant types includes 430 cultigens, and they distinguish minute differences in vegetative structures (Conklin, 1954). The organization of these categories can be investigated with techniques of ethnoscience (Berlin, Breedlove, and Raven, 1974). Europeans who lack this detailed fund of observations can make ludicrous mistakes. Colonial officials on the Jos Plateau in Northern Nigeria claimed that the Birom people were ignorant of the effects of fertilizer because they refused to put manure on their fields of acha (a *Digitaria* grass with tiny edible seeds). The fact is, however, that acha planted on enriched soil grows too quickly and falls over before its seed is ripe.

The practices of shifting cultivation are particularly adaptive to tropical conditions. Where temperatures and rainfall are high and no cold season intervenes, plants may grow all year round. The ecological cycle is typically rapid and shallow, with vegetation flourishing, falling or dying back, being rapidly decomposed by microorganisms, and then being reabsorbed by living plants. Nutrients are not significantly mixed with the soil, and continuous heat slows humus formation. Removal of the natural vegetation interrupts this cycle and leaves the earth with little fertility. Burning is an immediate way of converting the chemical components locked up in plants to a form in which they can be utilized by crops. To the degree that the soil is directly exposed to the action of rainfall and sunlight, its organic materials may rapidly be leached and the soil itself displaced by runoff. The best strategy is thus to keep the field protected with a series of differentially maturing crops in dense stands. The shifting cultivator in a rain forest may have, all in one place, food plants with subterranean tubers and root systems, ground vines, bushy vegetables, stalked plants, and trees with climbing vines. Forty separate crops have been seen growing in one Hanunóo swidden at the same time (Conklin, 1954). These successive levels break the force of the rain and shield the soil just as the natural vegetation would. All crops are not harvested at once, but rather the field is allowed to revert gradually to the original cover. "A natural forest has been transformed into a harvestable forest" (Geertz, 1963). A plot is abandoned when yields decline dramatically and labor input rises. This may result from the loss of nitrates or necessary minerals (especially potassium) in the soil (Nye and Greenland, 1950), but many authorities credit it to growing competition from weeds and to insect pests, which recover during the years following their destruction in the initial burning (de Schlippe, 1956, p. 214; Conklin, 1957; Carniero, 1961; Gourou, 1966, p. 37). Abandoning a field that has been farmed for two or three years allows a sufficient woody regrowth in the course of a ten-year fallow. Longer cropping and less time for natural regeneration may lead to a grass cover that provides less organic material, stores fewer minerals, doesn't suppress weeds, and with its dense mass of roots, makes for more difficult cultivation (Vasey, 1979).

Because of the special environmental limitations of tropical areas, certain agricultural tools and techniques of the temperate zone may be inappropriate. Because planting in the ashes among downed logs and branches does not require turning the soil over, a digging stick or dibble is quite adequate. In areas with a dry season, many trees need not even be cut. A fire built around the base is sufficient to kill them, and their bare branches do not impede the exposure of growing crops to sunlight. Fields are often left with some live standing trees to hasten their regeneration, and the complete clearing necessary for effective use of plows or mechanical power sources is seldom desirable in forest areas. Plows have been used effectively in deciduous forests or savannahs, but even in those locations care must be taken in some places not to break a sub-surface lateritic hardpan. Short-handled hoes do not run this risk, and they are also well adapted to lifting off a thin layer of topsoil and concentrating it in mounds or ridges on which crops can be planted. Use of large domestic animals for drawing plows and wagons and for provision of manure is limited to certain parts of the tropics by the prevalence of insect-borne diseases. Substitutes for shifting cultivation, such as green manuring and chemical fertilizer, have been proposed, but as long as adequate fallow periods can be maintained, this pattern remains the most efficient and proven method of agriculture in many of the world's tropical habitats.

Shifting cultivation demands a large amount of land per person because at any one time most of the arable area is being held as regenerating fallow. This means that population densities are characteristically low, seldom exceeding 150 per square mile, but it does not indicate that the system is inefficient. Cultivators may expend an average of only 500 to 1000 man-hours per year on crop production; their yields per unit of labor can equal or exceed those of some types of permanent agriculture (Harris, 1972). Where new land is available for the taking, shifting cultivators move frequently, cutting their swiddens out of primary forest. Pioneering groups tend to progress relatively rapidly in a linear fashion, as was probably characteristic of the Neolithic cultivators who expanded into temperate Europe (Harris, 1972). The frequent moves of settlers on the American frontier reflect a reliance on shifting methods and an unwillingness or inability to adopt the arduous stump removal, fencing, and animal husbandry that were necessary to make their clearings into farms. Where land is less readily available, a pattern of cyclic shifts in fields surrounding a village core may appear. Since accessible fields have sufficient time in fallow to avoid exhaustion, the settlement need never be relocated to a distant place

(Carniero, 1960). Where population density is particularly thin, as in many parts of the Amazon basin, the factor determining relocation may be less the lack of productive garden land than of wild game and fish that form the principal protein source in the Indian diet (Gross, 1975). The type of crop grown may also have implications for frequency of relocation. Seed crops such as rice or wheat are high in protein but make greater demands on the supply of nutrients in the ash and soil than do starchy root crops. Harris (1972) infers from this that grain-based shifting agriculture is less stable than vegeculture, requiring longer fallows and more frequent migrations.

SHIFTING AND INTENSIVE TECHNIQUES OF CULTIVATION

Though the principles and practices of shifting cultivation were unfamiliar to Westerners, they by no means exhausted the range of agricultural techniques found in the technologically simpler societies. In fact, a spectrum of systems exists, ranging in a series of intergrading types from constant movement into apparently virgin forest, as with the swiddening Iban of Borneo (Freeman, 1955), to intensive farming using irrigation to keep land in year-round production.* Table 1 compares the "paleotechnic peasant ecotypes" of the anthropologist Wolf (1966, pp. 20-21) with the types of land use outlined by the economist Boserup (1965, pp. 15ff.) and a classification of land or soil types in Africa offered by Allan (1965, p. 30). Wolf notes that long-term and sectorial fallowing both involve dibble or hoe cultivation, whereas short-term fallowing is often based on the plow and draft animals, as in Eurasian grain farming. Hydraulic systems allowing a permanent water supply make annual or continuous cropping possible. Boserup distinguishes between bush-fallow cultivation, in which brush and trees regrow during the fallow period, and short-fallow cultivation, in which only grasses come up during the resting phase. In the absence of modern methods, soils may limit the type of cultivation practiced. Allan points out that only shifting cultivation is possible on weak,

---

*Two wide-ranging recent surveys of African agriculture are Biebuyck (1963) and McLoughlin (1970).

TABLE 1.   TYPES OF LAND USE.

Type	Proportion of crop years to fallow years
Wolf	
Long-term fallowing	?
Sectorial fallowing	2-3 : 3-4
Short-term fallowing	1-2 : 1
Permanent cultivation	1 : 0
Boserup	
Forest-fallow	1-2 : 20-25
Bush-fallow	1-8 : 6-10
Short fallow	? : 1-2
Annual cropping	8-9 mos. : 3-4 mos.
Multicropping	1 : 0
Allan	
Shifting	1 : 10 or more
Recurrent	1 : 4-8
Permanent	1 : 2 or less

leached, or sandy soils, whereas volcanic or alluvial soils or strong red clays and loams in humid areas may support permanent use.

Though such typologies provide handy classifications, their suggestion of an evolutionary development of agriculture from simple shifting systems to complex intensive ones may obscure more basic functional relationships. It is by no means certain, for instance, that shifting agriculturalists hack their fields out of the woods because they lack improved farming tools and lack the knowledge of fertilizers, crop rotation, and irrigation. Anderson (1952) has postulated that some of the earliest domestication of plants may have taken place in "dawn gardens" on middens or refuse heaps near the campsites of hunter-gatherers. For people skilled in distinguishing minute differences in their environment, it would seem relatively easy to notice the more luxuriant growth of food crops on spots enriched by household wastes, droppings, or ashes. Even nonagriculturalists such as the Owens Valley

Paiute constructed simple dams and ditches to water patches of grass seeds on which they depended (Steward, 1938). The more we learn about indigenous agricultural methods, the more clearly it appears that food producers characteristically practice varieties of both shifting and intensive cultivation simultaneously. Though the main Zande fields are used for two or three years and then fallowed, smaller specialized plots are kept in long-term production. A ridge around the compound built up of household sweepings and topsoil scraped off the courtyard sustains a flourishing mixture of vegetables and grains. Men tend tobacco in moist beds under the overhanging roof thatch; women grow crops of maize, bananas, and cucurbits on refuse heaps. This type of kitchen gardening provides a partial but very important part of Zande subsistence (de Schlippe, 1956). The Gwembe Tonga formerly depended on alluvial fields annually inundated by the Zambezi River. These allowed permanent cultivation with no further fertilization. Land farther from the river, which was flooded less frequently, was correspondingly less fertile and less well watered; it produced only under a fallowing regime (Scudder, 1962). The Diola of Senegal have in recent years added the slash-and-burn cultivation of peanuts as a cash crop to their traditional intensive cultivation of wet-rice for subsistence purposes (Linares de Sapir, 1970). Permanent cultivation of favored plots with a fringe of sporadically used hinterlands is also familiar as the infield-outfield system along the Atlantic fringe of Western Europe (Wolf, 1966, p. 21). The infield near the house was level ground; its deeper soil was enriched by stable manure, straw, and household wastes. Poorer, steeper marginal fields could grow a crop of grain before returning to grass for hay or rough grazing.

The Kofyar of the Jos Plateau in Northern Nigeria have fields in concentric circles of diminishing intensity of land use. The homestead field, an acre or two surrounding each family residence (Plate 3), supports permanent plantings of intermixed sorghum, millet, cow peas, and leafy vegetables along with orchards of oil palms (Netting, 1968, pp. 55-107). No tool more complicated than the Sudanic hoe and the axe is used, and animal traction is unknown. In homestead fields on the hills, high walls of dry-laid stone retain terraced benches of level land. Runoff and erosion are further controlled by waffle-pattern ridging that catches and retains rainwater. The soil is rested only during three

Plate 3. *Kofyar homestead, Jos Plateau, northern Nigeria. The man is weeding the terraced, manured field of his homestead farm. Note the stone goat corral on the right where compost is collected. In the background are oil and giginya palms as well as other productive trees.*

months of the dry season; after that period compost from a goat corral is applied to the field. These methods, along with three annual hoeings, careful attention to growing crops, and selective harvesting, allow a family to derive its major subsistence year after year from the same plot. Other fields farther from the homestead are unmanured; they grow less demanding crops such as acha, peanuts, and sweet potatoes, and they are periodically rested. Bush fields outside the village perimeter are large tracts from which trees must be cut and grass turned under. After producing low-yielding crops of small grains or peanuts for six to nine years, these fields must be rested for twelve to fifteen years. The Kofyar are limited in the scale of their intensive agriculture by the availability of compost fertilizer. However, having a variety of field types with crops maturing at different times from June to December has significant advantages. It provides insurance against the failure of any one food source because of drought or insect depredations. Work is also spread out during the growing season, and the diet gains desirable variety.

Students of civilization have often attributed the development of intensive agriculture to revolutionary inventions such as metal tools, the plow, and domesticated draft animals (Childe, 1951), or to particular environments which challenged the creative powers of the inhabitants (Toynbee, 1947). Comparative evidence now suggests that many peoples practice intensive cultivation with rudimentary tools, and that the necessary knowledge need not be diffused from a few centers of cultural innovation but may be developed to meet localized needs. If most food producers have a repertoire of more and less intensive techniques, and if technology is not a crucial limiting variable, why do some groups rely largely on slash-and-burn while others systematically terrace, irrigate, fertilize, and rotate crops and seek in other ways to ensure permanent production from a piece of land? Considerable agreement now exists that, other things being equal, the agricultural system is functionally related to the density of local population and the resulting pressure on land resources. The ratio of population to arable land may change because of demographic growth within a confined area. People may be unable to move into new territories because of environmental limitations, such as the arid desert enclosing coastal valleys of Peru (Carniero, 1961) or a high-altitude cloud belt and lowered temperatures plus a lower zone of malarial infestation in Highland

New Guinea (Brookfield, 1964). In other cases the presence of hostile neighbors may prohibit expansion. The man/land balance may also change when the area of available land contracts because of changes in soil potential from erosion or salinization or because of loss to competing human groups. The less available land per capita, the more intensively it must be used. In a comparison of three Mexican communities, Palerm (1955) showed that slash-and-burn farmers use corn fields of only 1½ hectares each year, but a long fallow period requires that a total of 12 hectares be available for rotational use. In another village, fallow and crop time are approximately equal and small permanent gardens are also maintained; there, 2½ hectares are needed annually, but the total land necessary for a family is only 6½ hectares. Where irrigation permits two crops a year and the field is not rested at all, high continuous yields reduce the land requirement, both annual and total, to .86 hectare. Thus a given amount of land can support almost fourteen times as many families under an irrigated regime as the same area exploited by shifting techniques. Permanent intensive cultivation is a means of economizing as land resources become scarce.

If the type of agricultural system is indeed related to population pressure as Boserup (1965) and Dumond (1965) suggest, then changes in the man/land ratio should be reflected by an alteration in land use patterns. Archaeologists suspect that demographic growth may have rendered adaptive a progressive "settling in" of man into his environment—replacing big game hunting with more localized patterns of intensive collecting and encouraging experiments with domestication. Continued increases in population density would give a further selective advantage to intensive methods as opposed to shifting techniques, and there are indications that this was a key process in the development of civilization (Smith and Young, 1972). Contemporary evidence on change of this kind is available from West Africa. Kofyar intensive agriculture is correlated with a population density of about 300 per square mile (Netting, 1968, pp. 108ff.). In the past, the Kofyar were limited to a territory of about 200 square miles on or near the rugged escarpment of the Jos Plateau. The terrain protected them from slave raiders and from the mounted armies of surrounding city-states. Once this threat was removed by the colonially enforced peace, a fertile and largely empty plain to the south was opened to Kofyar exploitation.

Kofyar migrants grew many of the same crops there that they had at home and used only traditional tools, but they adopted shifting cultivation as they expanded into the new land (Plate 4). They killed the forest trees with fire and cropped their pioneer fields without fertilizer until production fell; the fields were then abandoned. Though yields per acre were less than on the traditional homesteads, the bush farms were five times as large (averaging 7.7 acres), and total production per farmer almost quadrupled. A change in the opposite direction, from shifting cultivation to manured kitchen gardens of root and vegetable crops under permanent orchards, has been noted among the Ibo of Eastern Nigeria. That transition has been most pronounced in areas of severe population pressure (400 to more than 1000 per square mile) and has followed a progressive shortening of the fallow period (Netting, 1969b).

The efficiency of labor may also vary in different agricultural systems. It has been hypothesized that intensive agriculture may conserve the scarce resource of land at the expense of a higher labor input for every unit produced (Boserup, 1965). Intensification requires more thorough cultivation and more frequent weeding, along with such permanent improvements as fencing, terracing, and the construction and maintenance of irrigation works. Work may be more tedious, and the food produced may have less variety and nutritive value (Clarke, 1966). Maintaining animals as a source of manure means that fodder and water must be provided daily for the stock. In temperate climates, hay and grain must be harvested and stored and barns or stables must be constructed to sustain the animals in the winter. Both the heavy initial labor investments and the necessity for continuous supportive agricultural activities may make intensive agriculture more expensive in terms of time than shifting cultivation. The actual hoeing, planting, and harvesting of a Kofyar homestead field does not require a vast amount of time, but the daily chores of caring for stall-fed animals must be included to arrive at total labor expenditure. When plentiful high-quality land becomes available—land that will grow crops without fertilizing, elaborate ridging, and capital improvements—shifting methods are recognized as more practical. In other areas where land has been freely available, as in frontier America, Brazil, and parts of southeast Asia, intensive farmers have normally adopted shifting tech-

Plate 4. *A voluntary work group of Kofyar migrant farmers. Cash crops of sorghum and millet are being hoed on forest land where the trees have been cut and burned. A drummer encourages the workers, who will be rewarded at the end of the day with beer.*

niques (Boserup, 1965, p. 62), not because they lack knowledge but because they economize by securing a higher return on their labor. Efforts to stimulate more intensive farming among the world's peoples must consider the possible decline in the labor efficiency of such methods and the resulting unwillingness of cultivators to adopt them.

Evolutionary models stressing ever-increasing human control of energy and the historic tendency to replace human labor by animal traction, machines, and fossil fuels would seem to require some revision in the light of the Boserup formulation. Though preindustrial agricultural change may have raised total output and increased yield per unit land, the cost in longer working hours and less productive labor may have been substantial. To evaluate this, we need more accurate calculation of land, labor, and production, both cross-culturally and through time in a single society. The gross correlation of increased population density with more intensive agricultural systems has now been found in West Africa (Gleave and White, 1969), Melanesia (Brookfield and Hart, 1971), Highland New Guinea (Brown and Podolefsky, 1976), Southeast Asia (Hanks, 1972), and the British Isles (Baker and Butlin, 1973), but lines of causation and the role of other factors are still unclear. A statistical comparison of twenty-nine groups of tropical subsistence cultivators shows that variation in population densities accounts for 58 percent of the variation in agricultural intensities (Turner, et al., 1977). It is apparent, however, that there are alternatives to agricultural intensification, and subsistence farmers may cope with population growth by migration, extension of cultivation into unsettled areas, accepting increasingly impoverished diets, or adopting crops with higher caloric yields (Grigg, 1979).

In a comparison of seventeen rice-growing societies of Asia, Hanks (1972) has shown that those who practice shifting cultivation average 31 people per square mile, those who broadcast the seed into naturally flooding river-valley fields average 255, and those who transplant their rice, irrigate and fertilize it, and produce several crops every year have an average population density of 988 per square mile. Yield per acre differs little between shifting and broadcasting but goes up considerably under the very intensive transplanting regime. As the farmer exerts more control over the spacing of plants, the timing of agricultural activities, and the application of water and nutrients, his yields show less annual variability. Labor input, however, does not rise in a simple association with intensity. Work directly connected with rice growing rises from 241 man-days per yearly crop under a shifting system to 292 for transplanting; broadcasting requires only 179. Indirect costs are also incurred for equipment, draft animals, and the rental or purchase of land. Whereas shifting cultivators need only axes, dibbles, and sickles, broadcasters must buy and feed water buffalo and make or purchase plows. Those who transplant rice must pay for expensive land, level and dike their fields, and dig and maintain a network of canals. When these costs, translated into man-days at the going rate for agricultural laborers, are added to direct labor input, the total cost rises at each greater level of intensity (Hanks, 1972, pp. 54-66). Efficiency does not decline, however. Broadcasting returns the most rice per man-day and shifting cultivation the least. People in lightly settled areas with multiple resources may choose to devote less labor to rice, spend more time fishing, hunting, and collecting, and avoid the heavy investment necessary for equipment and draft animals. Such decisions may result in both less work and less efficient labor at the same time. In parts of central Thailand, where in the last hundred years frontier shifting cultivation has given away to broadcasting and ultimately transplanting, a growing population on a fixed land base has had a narrowing range of agricultural options, pushing people in the direction of labor-intensive systems involving irrigation (Hanks, 1972, pp. 72-147).

The very factors of novelty, simplicity, and comprehensiveness that have made the Boserup hypothesis attractive to some archaeologists and cultural anthropologists (Spooner, 1972) have also made it a target for criticism. Bronson (1972) has argued that farmers may seek to minimize risk or increase their prestige, comfort, or health at the expense of labor efficiency. Social rewards may influence preferences, as when Thai rice growers regard cooperative work as pleasant but avoid solitary labor (Moerman, 1968). Intensification may be forced rather than voluntary, as an exploitative colonial regime imposes taxes and labor services (Geertz, 1963) or slavery is introduced by military coercion (Nell, 1972). The "carrot" of new economic opportunities may be as effective as the "stick" of population pressure in stimulating agricultural change. The history of Fukien province in China shows the coming of double cropping, market gardening, and cottage industry in areas accessible to coastal cities by water transport. The interior region, with similar population density, soils, and techniques, retained a relatively stagnant and less intensive agriculture (Rawski, 1972). Peasants were obviously responding to the appearance of desirable new goods and the chance to obtain them by selling food and crafts in the market.

If population growth is *a* factor rather than *the* factor leading to agricultural intensification, what causes this increase in numbers? Boserup (1965, p. 14) explicitly omits demographic explanations, phrasing her hypothesis in an "if . . . then" format. It is by no means proven that human populations always and everywhere show "the strong tendency to increase up to the point where serious shortages of important resources are in the offing . . . ," what Cowgill (1975) calls the "strictly from hunger" point of view of developmental processes. As discussed earlier in the case of hunter-gatherers, our current data are inadequate to demonstrate either the prevalence of self-regulation in prehistoric societies or the complex of nutritional, disease, and genetic changes that could lead to lowered mortality and/or increased fertility. Even very small annual increases in population work exponentially to generate surprisingly large populations in centuries (Cowgill, 1975); such steady or uninterrupted growth could not possibly have been characteristic of humankind. In fact, no one would contend that population has an inherent tendency to grow continuously or that intensification of agriculture is its sole and automatic outcome. An unfavorable person/land ratio in the savannah of northern Ghana has promoted a large-scale out-migration of males in search of wage labor (Hunter, 1966). Though it uses manuring and other intensive techniques, the indigenous system of compound farming has resulted in erosion and obvious soil degradation, while signs of malnutrition are evident in the people (Hunter, 1967).

Even when intensification does take place along the lines that Boserup suggested with higher labor input, more diversified cropping, and more manuring, it may not be sufficient to meet the needs of the most impacted rural populations or to prevent impoverishment of soils. A detailed comparison of three Ibo villages in eastern Nigeria (Lagemann, 1977) revealed declining production per acre in the most densely populated area and a compensating increase in education, off-farm employment in crafts and trade, and migration to cities. What Geertz (1963) has called "agricultural involution" in Java may lead to more work for less return and a declining standard of living for farmers. Agricultural system and population are certainly interacting ecological variables, but there is no reason to suppose that they adjust neatly and automatically at some new equilibrium level. The internecine warfare and feuding that characterized many autonomous tribal groups of cultivators was probably also related to over-population (Vayda, 1968), though the ecological connections are still obscure (Vayda, 1971; Netting, 1973). The presence of complex, reciprocal interactions among demographic growth, agricultural system, market economy, migration, and warfare should not dishearten the investigator. It is the nature of ecological thinking to cope with population parameters, resources, energy transfers, and competition at the same time. The controversies are at times frustrating and the lesson is painful, but it is one that anthropology is absorbing.

FUNCTIONAL LINKS BETWEEN FARMING AND SOCIAL ORGANIZATION

Agriculture impinges directly on social organization because people in groups do the work, share in the consumption of food, and have rights to the resources necessary for subsistence. In many farming societies the household is almost self-sufficient, and its structure is based on efficient labor mobilization and coordination. Whether the resident family tends to be a nuclear unit of father, mother, and children or is extended to include married pairs may depend on the nature of the tasks to be done. One village on the Fijian island of Moala showed a predominance of extended families because there were several widely separated food sources to be exploited. While some people were planting taro in one place, others were tending a distant coconut grove or gathering shellfish at another location. It was sensible to have these tasks allotted by a household head with central authority, who could also oversee the pooling of the various products and their redivision among family members (Sahlins, 1957).

Where cultivation is limited in scale but painstaking and careful, a nuclear family may provide all the necessary labor. Kofyar intensive homestead agriculture is carried on largely by the nuclear family, which is independent and responsible for its own support. Adding other household workers does not significantly increase production. Neighboring Plateau groups, such as the Angas and the Chokfem, show a preponderance of extended families, probably because the larger group of coresidents can rapidly cultivate the big fields characteristic of shifting agriculture. Such tracts cannot be effectively farmed piecemeal, so in the absence of mechanization the only way to hoe and plant a substantial area quickly at the most favorable point in the growing season is to call on a sizable force of workers. As land became more plentiful and the Kofyar reoriented themselves toward shifting cultivation, they also attempted to build up the available labor force by marrying more wives, extending their households by retaining married sons, staging more voluntary work parties with beer drinks (Plate 4), and hiring men by the day (Netting, 1968, pp. 202-203). The longer individual families stayed on the frontier and increased their production of cash crops, the bigger their households became. Whereas non-migrant Kofyar in the traditional homeland villages had a mean household size of 4.2, the domestic groups of those who had spent nine years or more as migrant farmers averaged 8.7 members (Stone, et al., 1984). Production was no longer limited by land scarcity in the new bush farms, but rather depended directly on the number of workers who could be mustered. An extended family also allowed the labor force to be divided during certain seasons so that both the home farm in the hills and the migrant farm on the plains could be tended. Once a more profitable cooperative enterprise became possible, young men who chafed under their fathers' administration of the restricted, intensively cultivated plots had less inducement to set up their own households. Intrafamily arguments about the division of the harvest also became less severe with growing abundance of food and cash.

Private ownership of the means of production has long been one of the sacred doctrines of many Western nations. Those who favor it and those who oppose it have both contrasted developed rights in property with a supposedly historically earlier and logically prior type of control that was communal and communistic, with lands, cattle, and tools held by the tribe or village. Ecologically-directed analyses have shown that rights to resources are not simply correlates of particular stages in social evolution, manifestations of cultural values, or legal creations. Rather, such rights are bound up with the way a resource is used and the degree of competition for it. In long-fallow shifting cultivation, an individual has very little use for a plot he once farmed but that now supports only wild vegetation as it regenerates. Individual fruit trees that he planted may remain in his possession, but otherwise his claim is gradually effaced once the land goes out of production. His rights are those of usufruct— of possessing the products of the land but not the land itself. If a plot is farmed again after twenty years, the original cultivator may be dead and new members of the community need land commensurate with their family obligations. Thus it is adaptive for a lineage group, ward, village, or subtribe to hold land as it were in common, assigning usufruct to its members according to their needs and protecting the fallow from outside trespassers. This allows easy adjustment to demographic fluctuations. A council or kin group of elders or a chief may decide on the allocation of plots each year. Such a system appears to work well with shifting agriculture. However, as population pressure introduces land scarcity and makes intensive methods increasingly desirable, group control of property encounters difficulties. There may not be enough good land to go around, and people grumble about their shares. More important, those who improve their land are unwilling to see it revert to some community pool. If a farm has been brought into annual production by the investment of labor in planting productive trees, manuring the soil, or digging irrigation channels, the rights of usufruct in effect become permanent (Netting, 1982a).

The traditional yam farming of the Ibo required a series of communally administered blocks around the village that were farmed in regular rotation. But in areas of dense population, the group could no longer guarantee to all of its members the use of an adequate supply of land. Under these circumstances, the small kitchen gardens adjoining each compound, which had always been individually held, were progressively expanded. Nuclear families who had previously lived in large extended households found it advantageous to separate themselves and go to live on plots that they could claim and proceed to improve (Udo, 1965). Land formerly assigned to any group member on a temporary basis was now held and inherited individually. Only thus could conflict over rights vital to subsistence be mitigated. Since the value of land was high, its permanent use could be acquired only by rent or sale—transactions that had no precedent in the past. Thus "availability of land determines the type of tenure . . ." (Chubb, 1961). The change does not result from legislation or other formal alteration of the rules but from a system of land exploitation in which higher investment, continuous productivity, and scarcity combine to make personal ownership an obvious solution. The switch from temporary to permanent use, accompanied by a change in agricultural methods and tenure, can come about very rapidly. A cash crop such as cacao or coffee, requiring long-term care and yielding over many years, tends to tie individuals to particular plots. Even a scarcity of agricultural land may anchor pastoralists to a particular area and set in motion individual claims to common lands, as in the case of the Kipsigis (Manners, 1964). In every society, some resources and tools are administered by groups and others are held wholly or in part by individuals. The relative proportions of public and private control cannot be understood apart from the use of these means of production and their permanency, dependability, productivity, and scarcity.

Impressive support for this interpretation comes from a statistical comparison of seventeen groups in the New Guinea highlands (Brown and Podolefsky, 1976). The peoples surveyed ranged from small linguistic and cultural units with low population density and shifting cultivation, such as the Siane and Maring, to large, densely populated groups such as the Chimbu, Enga, and Kapauku, who practice intensive sweet potato agriculture. Individual ownership of land as opposed to group ownership appears strongly correlated with both high population density and high agricultural intensity (Brown and Podolefsky, 1976, pp. 221-225). Higher population density is positively associated with the presence of such intensive methods as short or absent fallows, ground preparation using grids, mounds, or tillage, erosion and water control, and fertilization. These measures in turn are directly related to land holding: individual tenure occurs in all societies in which agriculture is permanent or the fallow period is less than six years, whereas group tenure is found with longer fallow periods. Though "group territory is recognized nearly everywhere, individual plots are held and inherited mainly where the fallow period is short and where trees and shrubs are planted by the owner" (Brown and Podolefsky, 1976,

Plate 5. A field of winter rye being harvested with a scythe and bound into sheaves by a family of Swiss farmers.

Plate 6. *Meadows on the Voralp above the village of Törbel in the canton of Valais, Switzerland. The lighter plots are individually-owned plots from which the hay has already been cut. The log buildings include both temporary quarters for the farm family and stalls with hay mows for their cattle.*

p. 221). Occupation and frequent cultivation set up recognized social claims to the lands as usufruct becomes in effect permanent (Netting, 1974). The question of whether population density or agricultural intensity is the independent variable is complex; the relationship certainly involves feedback links. A statistical association does not demonstrate the direction of causality, and the most tenable hypothesis may be that this relationship is interactional—that neither factor is consistently antecedent to the other (Brown and Podolefsky, 1976, p. 229).

The existence of individual tenure does not conflict with the maintenance of communal rights within the same community. For centuries residents of Törbel, a Swiss alpine village, bought, sold, rented, mortgaged, and inherited plots used as hay meadows, vineyards, grain fields, and vegetable gardens (Netting, 1976, 1981, pp. 57-69). Barns, granaries, cellars, and apartments in large log chalets are similarly owned (Plates 5 and 6). Other types of important property, however, are held by the corporate community and administered by an assembly of citizens with democratically elected officials. The high-altitude summer pasture or alp and the forests supplying fuel and building materials are communal possessions. Such rights not only assure all residents a share in grazing and wood but also protect and conserve essential resources. Trees that anchor soil on steep slopes and provide a shield against dangerous avalanches must be harvested selectively if they are to fulfill these functions and also give a sustained yield. The village council therefore decides what trees to cut each year and divides them into equal shares for which household heads draw lots. Similarly, all cattle owners are bound by the rule, first written down in the fifteenth century, that they may send only as many animals to the alp as they can support on hay during the long winter (Plate 7). This limits the total number of livestock and prevents overgrazing. Each owner has responsibility for work on walls, paths, and springs in proportion to the size of his herd. Tending and milking the cows and making cheese can be done by a small group of men, leaving the rest of the population free for making hay (Plate 8). Only individuals who were members of the village corporate community could pasture livestock on the alp or receive a share of firewood from the forest. Such rights of citizenship were inherited in the male line, and since the 1690s, Törbel has not admitted outsiders to legal membership,

Plate 7. Late in the spring, the cows are taken to summer grazing on the communal alp. The Swiss farmers are members of an alp association dating from the medieval period that limits the number of stock pastured on the alp, maintains the paths, and practices conservation of natural resources.

Plate 8. *A cheesemaker stirs the curds and whey in a copper kettle over an open hearth. Such traditional methods survive in only a few Swiss alpine communities.*

even if they bought private land in the village. Thus local political in-stitutions controlled potential in-migration leading to population growth and limited free access to community natural resources that were essential to a peasant livelihood (Netting, 1981, pp. 60-69). Communal control, equitable division, and careful conservation measures preserve necessary resources from reckless or selfish exploitation and avoid the "tragedy of the commons" often envisaged by biological ecologists (Hardin, 1968).

Chapter 6

TESTING ECOLOGICAL EXPLANATIONS

FIELD METHODS

Ecological hypotheses are relatively easy to put forward in anthropology. Proof that an ecosystem really works as postulated is much harder to come by. In the first place, ecological analysis requires different kinds of evidence from those anthropologists have usually collected. To understand effective factors in the physical environment may require an accurate knowledge of rainfall, subsurface water, soil types, temperatures, plant varieties, and animal types. Some data must be long-term in order to be meaningful: for example, the frequency and severity of drought and its effect on local flora and fauna are of crucial importance in determining the risks and advantages of hunting, herding, or farming in a particular area. An investigator cannot evaluate the decisions of a shifting cultivator until he can distinguish the succession of vegetation types in a regenerating field and the indications given by certain marker plants and tests of soil consistency that fertility has returned. Because the anthropologist may not have the necessary scientific background in climatology, geology, geography, or soil science, he may have to seek out available records or involve experts directly in his project. To plot Ifugao rice terraces and water sources, Harold Conklin (1980) has made extensive use of aerial photographs

and detailed contour maps made from them. He has also become a
practiced ethnobotanist by classifying the hundreds of useful plants
known to the Hanunóo. Richard Lee has enlisted the services of
archaeologists and nutritionists in his field studies of Bushmen and
has himself gathered detailed statistics on population composition and
distribution and on the ratio of labor input to food output (Lee, 1979).
Mapping and measuring of fields and weighing of harvested products
are arduous and time-consuming but necessary parts of the study of
any agricultural system (Netting, 1968, pp. 87-100). Some of these
tasks may be done by local enumerators, and where literate students
are available they can be trained to keep diaries of types and duration
of work effort in the household (Netting, 1969a; R. Dyson-Hudson,
1972) or the kind and amount of food consumed. However, such
record-keeping is difficult to maintain over a long period of time with
a representative sample and under sufficient supervision to prevent
a wide margin of error. Nevertheless, the contention of some anthropologists that it is not possible to collect quantifiable material of this
kind under field conditions is simply not true.

Some of the most convincing studies of environmental and economic
variables have been done practically unaided by anthropologists working in Highland New Guinea. Pospisil (1963) measured the area of
140 Kapauku gardens, carefully timed the various operations of the
agricultural cycle, and computed crop yields, even though this meant
weighing sweet potatoes almost every day as they were dug. These
data, along with household censuses, allowed him to correlate closely
the amount of land used by each household with the number of women
available for weeding, an activity that was thus shown to have key significance to total production. Pospisil's figures also indicated that
intensive complex cultivation was somewhat less efficient with respect
to labor than the extensive or shifting system practiced on mountain
slopes. Of particular interest was his demonstration that agricultural
labor time averaged 2.0 hours per day for males and 1.7 hours for
females, a finding that cast "serious doubt on the claim, so often made,
that native cultivation methods are wasteful, time-consuming, and economically inadequate" (Pospisil, 1963, p. 164).

A detailed, carefully controlled study of time expenditure made
among the Machiguenga shifting cultivators of southeastern Peru

indicates that men spend an average of 2.4 hours daily in their gardens and women contribute 0.9 hours. The hunting and collection of wild food occupies another 2 hours for adult married men and 0.9 hours for women, while manufacturing activities and food preparation also claim significant amounts of time. In this case quantification relied on random visits made over 134 days, resulting in 3495 observations of individuals. The data were processed by computer (Johnson, 1975). Rappaport (1967) has systematically assembled ecological evidence bearing on some suggestions of Vayda, Leeds, and Smith (1961) concerning the utility of the pig feast. Rappaport's appendices (1967, pp. 243-298) present in detail his method for estimating yields per unit area, energy expenditure in gardening, and carrying capacity. He outlines the floristic composition of primary forest and secondary growth as well as listing commonly propagated plants and nondomesticated resources. Rappaport investigated diet by the daily weighing of all vegetable foodstuffs brought home to four hearths of the Tsembaga over a ten-month period and then deducting the portion fed to pigs and the waste in preparation. The nutritional values of individual intakes could then be calculated. Translating the labor hours of clearing, fencing, planting, weeding, harvesting, and transporting tuber crops into kilocalories expended and comparing this to the caloric value of the crops produced allowed Rappaport (1971b) to demonstrate a favorable return on the human energy investment of sixteen to one. If, however, the sweet potatoes were fed to pigs for later consumption as pork, the input/output ratio was probably worse than one to one. Such data are absolutely necessary if anthropologists wish to understand the patterns of energy exchange central to the functioning of specific ecosystems.

CROSS-CULTURAL AND HISTORICAL COMPARISON

Crucial variations in adaptation may also be distinguished with the aid of comparative studies, both of contemporary societies and of the same group as it changes through time. The biological concept of niches has been used by Barth (1956) in analyzing the form and distribution of neighboring ethnic groups in North Pakistan. Different environmental zones are exploited by sedentary agriculturalist Pathans, farmer-herder Kohistanis, and nomadic pastoral Gujars. Pathans are confined to lower altitudes, where double-cropping can provide the surplus necessary to support a more highly developed economy and political organization. A more severe climate characterizes the high mountains, where the Kohistanis practice single-crop cultivation and transhumant herding. They were apparently driven into this less desirable area by the militarily stronger Pathans. Gujar nomads mingle symbiotically with both groups, trading milk, meat, and manure for food grains and other supplies. They act as a socially subordinate group, using pasture lands that cannot for various reasons be made productive by the local inhabitants. Differing political structure, community size, and social status characterize each people.

Relatively short-range and sometimes cyclic changes in the subsistence system and social organization of a single group may also be uncovered. Examples of this among the Kwakiutl and the Kofyar have already been given, and it is plain that the relationships of population, available resources, and social units of production and consumption may be altered rapidly, especially under the impact of disease, war, or new trade opportunities. Rappaport (1967) has documented among the New Guinea Tsembaga a recurring sequence involving several steps: growth in pig population, the necessity of bringing more land under cultivation, an increase in labor expended, and a scattering of house sites to bring people closer to outlying fields and to reduce interpersonal conflict. This cycle is completed by the ritual celebration of a pig festival in which large numbers of animals are slaughtered and community nucleation takes place. Settlement patterns thus appear to expand and contract in a "pulsating" process (Rappaport, 1967, pp. 68-70); and kinship groups may correspondingly vary from loose, cognatic clan clusters to more rigidly bounded, agnatic descent groups (1967, p. 26). Viewed without a time perspective, the community form and kinship organization at any specific period might be taken as "traditional" and unchanging, thus blurring their intimate adjustment to other factors in the ecology. This type of analysis is also helpful in showing how population density and land scarcity may trigger the outbreak of warfare among groups that were previously fusing (Rappaport, 1967, p. 116).

Perhaps the most thoroughgoing application of the comparative-historical approach to ecological studies is John Bennett's study (1969) of a region in western Canada. Bennett contrasted Indians, ranchers, farmers, and Hutterites, both in terms of their current strategies of converting the natural environment into resources of subsistence and profit and also as they have adapted historically to their terrain, their national economy, and each other. The statistical and chronological data available for such purposes in a modern literate society are extensive. Bennett draws on a 60- to 70-year period of settlement that includes rapid in-migration, economic depression, and the coming of railroads, automobiles, and telephones, all of which influence population size and dispersion, settlement location, and the differing status of social groups. Recollections, government records, and legal documents allow the correlation of individual family growth, development of the farming enterprise, and external fluctuations of climate and the market economy (Bennett, 1969, p. 229). Indeed, political and economic forces not under local control, such as homesteading laws and the price of wheat, may be more important factors in the ecology of modern, specialized cash farming than the vagaries of rainfall.

In commenting on successive orientations of anthropological theory, we have frequently contrasted an approach emphasizing cultural values with an ecological framework. Bennett achieves a fruitful synthesis by considering the reasons for the differing attitudes toward nature held by ranchers and farmers (1969, p. 94) and by discussing the origins of the high prestige of ranching and its associated symbols.

HUMAN PROBLEMS AND THE RELEVANCE OF ECOLOGICAL RESEARCH

Within the academic discipline of anthropology, the significance of a theory or interpretation often depends on whether fellow specialists can be persuaded of its validity. An attractive or novel idea is one that makes sense of disparate and previously unrelated facts. The formulation that appears more comprehensive, parsimonious, and elegant is accepted. Research findings that seem consistent are seldom checked by other scientists, restudies are rare, and there is no laboratory situation for experimental manipulation of the data of human ecology. People whose jobs involve making administrative decisions or coping with changing land use, health systems, marketing, or rights to resources often find anthropological information irrelevant or overly abstract. But it is about just such matters that anthropologists claim special knowledge.

Ecologically-oriented research has the potential of speaking directly to contemporary concerns with environmental degradation, energy supplies, pollution, and social disorganization. Proposed changes must be examined before they are implemented, and means such as environmental and cultural impact statements have been developed to do this. Anthropologists need not confine themselves to pessimistic though instructive accounts of how modernization goes awry (Spicer, 1952) or why grandiose governmental schemes flounder (Reining, 1966). Their familiarity with social systems and value patterns, united with data on production, population, energy transfers, and information flows, can contribute to the modelling of whole systems and predictions of the causes and characteristics of change.

Intelligent planning requires the input of social science, and ecological anthropologists must accept this as both a responsibility and a challenge. Moreover, action or applied research carries the opportunity for actually testing our hypotheses. The "proof of the pudding" is not solely its intellectual digestibility. In the real world we can judge whether postulated relationships between disease and settlement pattern or between land availability and agricultural intensity exist as something more than imaginary constructs. The success or failure of medical programs, local government activities, and agricultural innovations we recommend can be measured objectively in terms of the physical and economic well-being of those people affected. As formerly self-sufficient Papua New Guineans voluntarily and enthusiastically embark on growing coffee and raising beef cattle, their neglect of food gardens and their purchase of bottled beer may make them vulnerable to market price fluctuations, declining dietary quality, and environmental damage (Grossman, 1981, 1984). To the extent that long-term observations are initiated and continuing re-evaluations of research results and predictions are carried on, as in the study of Tonga displaced by the Kariba Dam (Scudder and Colson, 1972), significant change in entire ecosystems can be reliably charted.

The most explicit contemporary call for "a policy-relevant cul-

tural ecology" has been sounded by John Bennett (1976, p. 3).
The limited impact of ecological research by anthropologists can be
traced to these factors:

1.   Anthropologists have been concerned primarily with
      societies in the distant past, or in remote locations, where
      impact on the environment often, or usually, has been
      minimal.

2.   Many if not most existing studies have treated the societies
      as isolates (whether they are or not) out of contact with
      larger institutional systems. Hence, in such cases, the
      study of the role of powerful forces external to these com-
      munities in molding their use and abuse of environment
      has not been considered.

3.   The majority of cultural-ecological studies of living societies
      have been concerned with culture rather than ecology: sub-
      sistence systems are described, but the major emphasis is
      on their contribution to an explanation of sociocultural
      forms.

4.   Few communities have been studied over sufficient periods
      of time to enable cultural anthropologists to determine the
      pattern of growth and change in resource use; hence there
      is a tendency to conceive of ecological relations as rela-
      tively stable and enduring. (Bennett 1976, p. 26)

The need for new priorities is emphasized by a combination of
shrinking chances for conventional fieldwork in many parts of the
Third World, the encouragement of research on national needs in
the industrialized countries, and such well-publicized, immediate
ecological problems as the energy crises (Pimental et al., 1973),
drought and food shortages (Caldwell, 1975, Torry, 1984), deforestation
and erosion, and overpopulation (Demeny, 1974).

The understanding of local ecosystems already achieved and the
models proposed for the interaction of landscape, subsistence techniques, population, and social organization are clearly basic to any
advice and predictions the anthropologist can offer. "Pure" and

applied research can and should be mutually reinforcing (cf. Bennett, 1976, p. 32). In a good example of this approach, Clarke (1976) summarizes our rapidly accumulating knowledge of the processes by which shifting cultivation is maintained in the tropical forest (see above, p. 61), but goes on to deal with cases in which fallows are shortened, forest regeneration fails, and the balanced swidden system breaks down. In Papua New Guinea, not all groups practice the selective weeding and tree planting that promote the regrowth of trees, and less productive grasslands are actually maintained by indiscriminate burning. There is no reason for assuming that a technologically simple society lives in a state of equilibrium with its environment or that the continuation of practices that worked in the past will be adaptive in the future. Moreover, internal and external changes affecting the system cannot be avoided. Given the suppression of warfare and better medical care and transport facilities, population growth is a foregone conclusion. Shortened fallows, declining yields, poorer nutrition, incursions on primary forest, land degradation, and increased labor requirements are predictable results. At the same time, subsistence needs for land are considerably increased by cash-cropping demands as local farmers take one of the few ways open to them for participation in a market economy. To ease the transition from shifting to permanent cultivation, Clarke (1976) suggests the official encouragement of the most effective native means of intensification. These include the promotion of crop diversity within a single garden rather than monoculture (cf. Igbozurike, 1971), the planting of arboreal fallows, the use of erosion control devices and agricultural terracing, and emphasis on sustained-yield tree crops. Science and industry can contribute by breeding tropical plants to raise yields and protein content, experimenting with fallow systems and cultivation methods, and developing improved low-energy tools and trace-element fertilizers (cf Schumacher, 1973). Livestock might also be incorporated into crop-grass or crop-legume rotations. Rather than advocating blanket substitution of temperate zone methods, high-energy technology, and factory-farm or plantation organization, Clarke recommends creative and practical solutions embodying the proven responses of generations of tropical agriculturalists as furthered by the insights of modern science. Given the tremendous speed of change and of population growth, such adjustments may not be possible, but they indicate the value of an ecological perspective on a significant human dilemma.

Recent research in the Amazon basin indicates that the chemical deficiences of tropical soils can be identified and remedied, allowing intensive systems of continuous cultivation (Sanchez, et al., 1982). Slash and burn methods of land clearance both add nutrients in ash and avoid the topsoil compaction and displacement that results from bulldozing. Growing three crops a year as rotations of upland rice, corn, and soybeans or upland rice, peanuts, and soybeans keeps the ground covered most of the year as protection against rain. Monoculture of the same crops could not produce similarly sustained yields because of a build-up of plant diseases and pests. A complete fertilizer compensated for soil deficiencies in phosphorus and potassium and declines during cropping in nitrogen, calcium, magnesium, and a number of trace elements (Sanchez, et al., 1982, p. 824). Thus key elements of shifting cultivation practice including burning, hand tillage, maintaining a protective mantle of vegetation, and crop rotation have been effectively combined with chemical fertilizers to intensify the use of tropical areas without environmental degradation. Such economically feasible methods are unlikely to be adopted, however, unless markets are accessible and agricultural products can command attractive market prices (Sanchez, et al., 1982, p. 827).

Americans, accustomed to thinking of Cyrus McCormick, Thomas Edison, and the Wright brothers as patron saints of an irresistable, beneficent technological progress, sometimes find it difficult to envision the human confusion and misery which may also flow from labor-saving inventions and life-preserving scientific discoveries. The Green Revolution provides a cautionary tale of unanticipated consequences. There is no question of the need for higher food production, particularly in the poorer and more crowded parts of the earth. The breeding of better-yielding strains of wheat and rice was an impressive effort to meet this need. But this agricultural intensification, like any other, also involved costs—irrigation systems had to be extended, wells drilled, and gasoline-powered pumps installed and serviced. The new grains can be produced at full capacity only with a substantial infusion of hard cash. Without power, chemical fertilizers, and pesticides, the new crop varieties were vulnerable to environmental hazards (Bodley, 1976). The farmer thus became dependent on manufactured goods he could not produce and ultimately on fossil fuels available only at ever higher world market prices.

To take advantage of the new methods, a farmer should own land and be able to invest existing capital in seed, pumps, fertilizer, insecticides, and the rental of tractors and threshing machines. Areas in which such techniques are feasible and where the inputs are available show spiralling land prices. Thus in Bihar State, India, professionals, merchants, and large landowners have found profits in agriculture, but the overwhelming majority of small landholders lack the resources to adopt the technology. Even a seven-acre farm requires a pair of bullocks worth Rs 2000, a tube-well costing about Rs 6500, and other inputs of Rs 1500, or a total of Rs 10,000 (Ladejinsky, 1969). Poor farmers cannot get loans for such amounts, and the small sums they acquire from local moneylenders must be repaid with 75 percent annual interest.

Cooperative credit societies require only 8 to 9 percent interest, but their loans are small and given mostly to farmers with larger-than-average-sized plots. Sharecroppers who must supply all tools, seeds, labor, and other costs of making a crop have no security of tenure rights enforceable by a court of law. Large owners attempt to evict them in order to modernize methods, streamline production, and employ cheaper hired labor. Because of the large number of landless wage workers, Bihar male laborers receive only Rs 2-3 plus one or two meals a day (Ladejinsky, 1969). Although dramatic increases in yield per acre and in total food production can be credited to the Green Revolution, the disparity of incomes between the rural rich and poor is unquestionably growing. With a 22 percent increase in the Bihar rural population between 1951 and 1961, land hunger is growing, the average fragmented three-acre holding continues to shrink, and 23 percent of landowners control 68 percent of the land (Ladejinsky, 1969). Legal limits on maximum farm size are routinely evaded by large proprietors with the help of government officials.

Wolf Ladejinsky, an American agricultural economist with extensive experience in the postwar land reform of Japan and Taiwan, recognized the necessity for the technological improvements of the Green Revolution, but he also insisted that this change should be a benefit rather than a new burden for the peasant cultivator. Rather than considering production or food supply in isolation, he placed these factors firmly in a comprehensive ecological matrix emphasizing the role of social arrangements and the distribution of economic costs and rewards.

> It is not the fault of the new technology that the credit service does not serve those for whom it was originally intended; that the extension services are not living up to expectations; . . . that security of tenure is a luxury of the few; that rents are exorbitant; that ceilings on agricultural land are notional; that for the greater part tenurial legislation is deliberately mis-carried; or that wage scales are hardly sufficient to keep body and soul together. These are manmade institutional inequities. Correcting all of them within the foreseeable future is out of the question. On the other hand, even if only some of them are dealt with—security of tenure, reasonable rent and credit to sustain production needs—a measure of economic and social justice could be fused with economic necessity, thereby adding another dimension to the Green Revolution (Ladejinsky, 1969).

Since the late 60s, the Indian sub-continent has served as a great proving ground for Green Revolution technology, and anthropologists have been able to apply their holistic but at the same time ethnographically specific methods to communities experiencing this major transformation. Murray Leaf's (1972, 1984) studies of a rual Sikh community in the north Indian Panjab document a history of successful agricultural intensification involving technological, economic, and social changes. Electric and diesel pumps on both new tube wells and traditional shaft wells made possible the quadrupling of water lifting capacity from a water table that was actually rising due to percolation from an irrigation canal system (Leaf, 1984, pp. 38-42). Improved seed and chemical fertilizer, along with the assured water supply raised yields of wheat and maize and allowed adoption of transplanted rice. Farmers began to use herbicides and pesticides and to rely on agricultural advice from university research. Rainfall-dependent crops declined as did the need for fallowing. Fodder for domestic animals was no longer scarce, so the village stall-fed cattle and buffalo population could increase, providing higher milk production and more compost for the fields (Leaf,

1984, p. 58). Both the local diet and market sales of crops were further improved by grain storage in metal drums. Cooperative credit facilities and income from family members in off-farm occupations allowed the purchase of land and, in a few cases, tractors.

Critics of the Green Revolution have emphasized the obvious growing rural dependency on industrial inputs, but the private profitability of increased participation in the market has been shown by Sikh farmers' eager adoption of the dependable new methods. Over the 1965 to 1978 period, tenancy has almost disappeared and the number of landowning families is up. The predicted further immiseration of the poor has not taken place in the Panjab. Agricultural laborers have modestly improved hourly rates, but employment days per year have increased dramatically with greater demands for plowing, weeding, and harvesting together with more construction of houses, wells, and roads (Leaf 1984, p. 132). In fact, the village has attracted landless people whose rising incomes have allowed them to acquire new skills and education. The problems of change are not those of peasant inefficiency or irrationality as Leaf so cogently demonstrates. Cultural continuity in kinship and household organization, religion, and political competition support rather than impede rapid economic innovation. Obstacles more often lie in the resources provided to villagers from larger social systems – the inappropriate technologies, the lack of basic facilities like roads and electricity, and the failure to deliver the new agricultural inputs at needed places and times, in the right amounts, and on reasonable terms (Leaf, 1984, p. 256). Leaf (1984, p. 141) gives part of the credit for Green Revolution successes in higher production and better local living standards to government officials "who at last seem to understand and respect the villagers and who provide incentives that will attract the farmers' interest and activity instead of demands that farmers will have to ignore or resist."

Given the complexity of local ecosystems and their necessary incorporation in an ever expanding network of regional, national, and global influences, it is misleading to give pat answers on why the Green Revolution should be more effective in Panjab than Bihar, or why Javanese agriculture became involuted in contrast to the dynamism of Japan (Geertz, 1963). The dogmatic assertions and quick technological fixes of macro-economic modernization models and dependency theories are equally unsatisfying. An ecological approach rests firmly on the empirical description of functionally related factors in a particular living community, it places these variables in the context of an inclusive political-economy, and it seeks to achieve valid generalizations through controlled comparison, cross-sectional analysis of groups in a relatively homogeneous area, and longitudinal studies of change through time (Gross, 1984). The legs of this social science tripod may never be equally sturdy or complete, but they provide our best chance for an understanding that is relevant to significant contemporary events in the real world.

THE LIMITATIONS OF ECOLOGY

In an effort to stress the positive scientific advantages of ecological analysis in cultural anthropology, I have certainly neglected both the limitations of the method and the claims of alternative modes of understanding human society. If we are to avoid the oversimplifications of environmental determinism or any other determinism, we must recognize the unanswered questions. Cultures do not normally reach the best of all possible solutions to the problems of livelihood and shelter; rather they strike one of a number of potentially viable compromises. We know that within a society, individuals make choices in an effort to maximize their satisfactions, but we are able to discern only dimly what factors materially influence these decisions. Most important, no one ever adapts to environmental circumstances in a wholly unbiased, rational, and calculating manner. The culture each of us inherits is a summation of coping devices that have proved their worth in the past, but they may not be equally effective in the present. Personality structure, configurations of values, and systems of cognition relate to subsistence success in ways we cannot yet fully fathom. Cultural identities, languages, dress, religion, and marriage customs continue to differentiate ethnic groups who utilize exactly the same environment in nearly identical ways (Freilich, 1963).

Recent work on adjoining German- and Romance-speaking communities in the Italian Alps indicates substantial cultural differences persisting over centuries despite a common ecological pattern of mixed mountain agriculture (Wolf, 1962; Cole, 1969). In the past, each household needed access to plowland, meadows, and forest at various altitudes to remain viable, and the supply of these land types was strictly limited by the topography. Without sufficient land for support, a man could not marry and found a family; instead, he either remained a bachelor member of a sibling's household or emigrated.* The German-speaking village practiced impartible inheritance, with the eldest son acquiring all of his father's holding. The preference in the neighboring Romance-language village was for all children to share equally in the land of their parents. One method would appear to preserve a holding intact, while the other would fragment it in each generation. In fact, however, both ideologies of inheritance are modified to conform to territorial and social limitations. The system of primogeniture is often bypassed when friction between father and eldest son causes the latter to leave and a younger heir to be chosen; and under the partible rule, the heirs either operate the holding together or turn over managerial control to one of their number, who attempts to buy out the shares of the rest. "Sharing common ecological and economic problems, these villages of diverse origin have converged on a single adaptive solution to the problem of how to manage the intergenerational transfer of right to land. In spite of their differing ideologies, the size of holding and the composition of the domestic units show remarkable similarity in both villages" (Cole, 1970). Inheritance rules must be traced to historical causes, but the actual inheritance process is determined by the ecological setting. The importance of cultural differences is not lost in this situation, however. When these isolated communities were opened by roads and new wage labor opportunities became readily available in the cities, many Romance-speaking youths deserted their village permanently, while their contemporaries among the Germans took industrial jobs in order to return home, buy land, and engage in commercial milk production (Cole, 1969). Environment and technology viewed apart from cultural ideology and social structural prescriptions are obviously insufficient to account for the different directions taken by change.

The thrust of ecological inquiry is to distinguish more adequately

---

*For a Norwegian case in which introduction of a new resource created problems of access that could only be handled by changes in marriage and inheritance patterns, see Brox (1964).

those features of social organization and cultural values that are closely related to the human use of the environment as opposed to those that are less relevant. Steward points to this distinction in his designation "culture core" (1955, p. 37). Returning to the classic ethnographic case of ecological interpretation, David Damas (1969a) has compared three Eskimo groups with regard to both environmental adaptation and historical processes. Common methods of exploiting the environment among Copper, Netsilik, and Iglulik Eskimos seem to be directly related to the size of the winter aggregations. All three groups harpoon seals through the ice. This method works best when a large number of hunters participate in order to cover a higher proportion of the breathing holes in a given area. Therefore, winter camps tend to have 50 to 150 persons, while the less cooperative summer activities promote smaller, more mobile task groups. The Iglulik, with their greater concentration on sea-mammal hunting, appear to have a somewhat more secure subsistence base that obviates infanticide and allows kin exogamy. In the other groups, where survival is harder, female infanticide is practiced and the resulting limited choice of marriage partners leads to marriage between relatives. Other things vary in ways that have little apparent relation to the food quest, however. The Copper Eskimo area is characterized by nuclear family organization, whereas the economically similar Netsilik have extended families like the Iglulik. Certain contrasts of kinship terminology also exist within single exploitative zones, and it would appear that this trait, so beloved of anthropologists, is not always very relevant ecologically. Kinship terms may indeed be a conservative part of social organization, with changes in these terms lagging behind alterations in group composition and marriage as Murdock (1949) has claimed. Where social features are not congruent with exploitative patterns, historical explanations of migration, diffusion, or drift may be introduced. Historical controls help us to focus on those factors in culture and society that allow for viable alternatives rather than demanding one specific ecological adaptation.

A continuing danger confronting cultural ecology is the tendency among some anthropologists to see it as reductionist calorie counting, mindless number crunching, or vulgar materialism. A symbolic or structuralist conception of culture as meaningful order is often contrasted to culture as a means of meeting biological needs or as a trivial epiphenomenon of economic action and "practical reason" (Sahlins, 1976). The simple and oftimes compelling answers to such riddles of culture as the sacred cow or the pork taboo that emerge from the "demo-techno-econo-environmental determinism" of Marvin Harris (1974, 1977) are seen as denials of cultural distinctiveness and the abundant evidence of maladaptive behavior in human societies. Though Harris (1969) concedes that the strategy of cultural materialism does not predict the evolution of every society or provide law-like as opposed to probabilistic statements, he derides as eclectic, middle-range, contradictory, and idiographic just the kinds of detailed, systematic, particularistic ethnographic analyses that most ecologists do.

Claims to exclusive knowledge that pit the good-guy scientific empiricists against the literary and philosophical mentalists are bound to arbitrarily limit the scope of inquiry and substitute an artificial dichotomy for an appreciation of different paths to truth. Academic polemics from both sides deny the holism that has been a fundamental orientation of anthropology since its beginnings (Netting, 1982b). Rappaport's (1967) hypothesizing of systematic articulation between the Maring ritual cycle of killing pigs for the ancestors and the local production system of land, labor, population, and subsistence does not require that either economic elements or religious beliefs be logically causal or temporally prior to the other. Ecological factors never operate in a cultural vacuum nor do the enduring patterns of language, kinship, and cultural values that every individual inherits prevent adaptation to a material environment. Ecological anthropologists, by and large, assert the possibility of a scientific, empirical understanding of instrumental behaviors in a material world without disengaging this behavior from the symbols, precepts, and preferences that constitute an encompassing intellectual, ideological sphere.

Among those who carry on ecological research, there is no necessary concensus on important theoretical issues. There have been debates about the modeling of human ecosystems using the methods of biological ecology and focusing on populations rather than cultures (Vayda and Rappaport, 1968; Bennett, 1976). Such borrowed terms as adaptation, niche, and carrying capacity can be more precisely applied by anthropologists as demonstrated by Hardesty (1977), Brush (1975), and Orlove (1980). A vigorous new literature is now growing up around the use of optimal foraging models for hunter-gatherers (Winterhalder and Smith, 1981). The attempt to specify and quantify energy flows and nutrient pathways using schematic diagrams (Rappaport, 1971b; Little and Morren, 1977) has encountered problems of reliable data collection in the field (Ellen, 1982, pp. 95-122) and provides little insight into human variation in resource use in given localities (Moran, 1984, p. 12). Indeed the entire concept of the ecosystem, though seen as heuristically useful, is now criticized as reifying the system as if it were a biological organism, overemphasizing stability at the expense of structural change through time, and lacking clear criteria for boundary definition (Moran, 1984, p. 14). The homeostatic equilibrium models used to describe the complex cybernetic operations of feed-back and self regulation (Odum, 1971) are now seen as restricting our understanding of structural change and evolution responding to natural selection (Richerson, 1977; Smith, 1984). Social and technological responses to specific environmental events, including demographic, economic, and political events in regional or international systems, may bring about major cumulative changes (Vayda and McCay, 1975; Lees and Bates, 1984). An earlier neofunctionalist ecology must be given time depth by examining interacting variables as they change historically (Orlove, 1980; Netting, 1981, 1984). The possibility that rapid population growth with accompanying exhaustion of fuel resources, chemical pollution, soil degradation, food shortages, and vastly destructive conflict could cause irreversible damage to the entire ecology of humankind warns us against any easy confidence in the adaptive success of our species.

Ecological studies in anthropology have only begun to realize their potential; but it is already obvious that these studies arise not from a new dogma but from an attempt to widen existing perspectives in the science of man.* As our dependence on the physical environment and the effects of disturbing intricately functioning ecosystems become more critically apparent, we need to know more about the varieties of long-standing, successful human adaptation. It is both possible and necessary to gather empirical data on operating social groups, describing

---

*Representative articles using an ecological or adaptational approach to cultural study are available in collections edited by Cohen (1968), Damas (1969), Vayda (1969), and Burnham and Ellen (1979).

their technology of production and protection, distinguishing the variables that are effective in their surroundings, and assembling reliable quantitative profiles of population, labor input, rights to resources, and consumption. To do this, anthropologists must learn some new skills and call on other sciences for expert help. We must share an endeavor that radically transcends disciplinary boundaries. To be convincing, our findings require not only correlations leading to logical functional explanations, but also cross-cultural comparisons and evidence of historical change. Seen in this perspective, the ways of hunter-gatherer subsistence, the Northwest Coast potlatch, the East African cattle complex, and changing agricultural systems become perhaps a little clearer. With the ecological approach, the traditional concerns of anthropology for cultural values and social organization take on a new dimension and a fresh excitement.

REFERENCES

Abruzzi, W. S. (1980). "Flux among the Mbuti Pygmies of the Ituri Forest: An Ecological Interpretation." In Eric B. Ross, ed., *Beyond the Myths of Culture: Essays in Cultural Materialism.* New York:Academic Press. Pp. 3-31.

Adams, J. W. (1973). *The Gitksan Potlatch: Population Flux, Resource Ownership and Reciprocity.* Toronto: Holt, Rinehart and Winston of Canada.

Adams, J. W. (1981). "Recent Ethnology of the Northwest Coast." *Annual Review of Anthropology* 10:361-392.

Allan, W. (1965). *The African Husbandman.* Edinburgh: Oliver and Boyd.

Ammerman, A. J. (1975). "Late Pleistocene Population Dynamics: An Alternative View." *Human Ecology,* 3: 219-233.

Anderson, E. (1952). *Plants, Man, and Life.* Boston: Little, Brown.

Anderson, J. N. (1974). "Ecological Anthropology and Anthropological Ecology." In J. J. Honigmann, ed., *Handbook of Social and Cultural Anthropology.* Chicago: Rand McNally. Pp. 477-497.

Arensberg, C. M. (1963). "The Old World Peoples." *Anthropological Quarterly,* 36: 75-99.

Aschmann, H. (1965). "Comments." In A. Leeds and A. P. Vayda, eds., *Man, Culture, and Animals.* Washington, D.C.: American Association for the Advancement of Science. Pp. 259-270.

Baker, A. R., and R. A. Butlin (1973). *Studies of Field Systems in the British Isles.* Cambridge: Cambridge University Press.

Barnard, A. (1979). "Kalahari Bushman Settlement Patterns." In D. C. Burnham and R. F. Ellen, eds., *Social and Ecological Systems.* New York: Academic Press. Pp. 131-144.

Barnard, A. (1983). "Contemporary Hunter-Gatherers: Current Theoretical Issues in Ecology and Social Organization." *Annual Review of Anthropology* 12:193-214.

Barnett, H. (1938). "The Nature of the Potlatch." *American Anthropologist,* 40: 349-358.

Barth, F. (1956). "Ecologic Relationships of Ethnic Groups in Swat, North Pakistan." *American Anthropologist,* 58: 1079-1089.

Bates, M. (1953). "Human Ecology." In A. L. Kroeber, ed., *Anthropology Today.* Chicago: University of Chicago Press. Pp. 700-713.

Benedict, R. (1946). *Patterns of Culture.* New York: New American Library. (First published 1934.)

Bennett, J. W. (1969). *Northern Plainsmen: Adaptive Strategy and Agrarian Life.* Chicago: Aldine.

Bennett, J. W. (1976). *The Ecological Transition: Cultural Anthropology and Human Adaptation.* Oxford: Pergamon.

Berlin, B., D. E. Breedlove, and P. H. Raven (1974). *Principles of Tzeltal Plant Classification.* New York: Academic Press.

Bicchieri, M. G. (1969). "The Differential Use of Identical Features of Physical Habitat in Connection with Exploitative, Settlement, and Community Patterns: The Bambuti Case Study." In D. Damas, ed., *Ecological Essays.* Ottawa: National Museums of Canada, Bulletin No. 230. Pp. 65-72.

Biebuyck, D., ed. (1963). *African Agrarian Systems.* London: Oxford University Press.

Binsford, L. R. (1968). "Post Pleistocene Adaptations." In L. R. Binford and S. R. Binford, eds., *New Perspectives in Archaeology.* Chicago: Aldine.

Bishop, C. A. (1970). "The Emergency of Hunting Territories among the Northern Ojibwa." *Ethnology,* 9: 1-15.

Bishop, C. A. (1972). "Demography, Ecology, and Trade among the Northern Ojibwa and Swampy Cree." *Western Canadian Journal of Anthropology,* 3: 58-71.

Bishop, C.A. (1978). "Cultural and Biological Adaptations to Deprivation: the Northern Ojibwa Case." In C. D. Laughlin and I. A. Brady, eds., *Extinction and Survival in Human Populations.* New York: Columbia University Press. Pp. 208-230.

Boas, F. (1888). "The Central Eskimo." *Bureau of American Ethnology, Sixth Annual Report,* pp. 409-669.

Boas, F. (1921). "Ethnology of the Kwakiutl." *Bureau of American Ethnology, 35th Annual Report,* Parts 1 and 2.

Bodley, J. H. (1976). *Anthropology and Contemporary Human Problems.* Menlo Park, Calif.: Cummings.

Boserup, E. (1965). *The Conditions of Agricultural Growth.* Chicago: Aldine.

Breman, H., and C. T. de Wit (1983). "Rangeland Productivity and Exploitation in the Sahel." *Science* 221:1341-1347.

Bronson, B. (1972). "Farm Labor and the Evolution of Food Production." In B. Spooner, ed., *Population Growth: Anthropological Implications.* Cambridge: MIT Press. Pp. 190-218.

Bronson, B. (1975). "The Earliest Farming: Demography as Cause and Consequence." In S. Polgar, ed., *Population, Ecology, and Social Evolution.* The Hague: Mouton.

Brookfield, H. C. (1964). "The Ecology of Highland Settlement: Some Suggestions." In J. B. Watson, ed., *New Guinea: The Central Highlands.* Special Publication, *American Anthropologist,* 66 (4, Pt. 2): 20-38.

Brookfield, H. C., and D. Hart (1971). *Melanesia: A Geographical Interpretation of an Island World.* London: Methuen.

Brown, P., and A. Podolefsky (1976). "Population Density, Agricultural Intensity, Land Tenure, and Group Size in the New Guinea Highlands." *Ethnology,* 15: 211-238.

Brox, O. (1964). "Natural Conditions, Inheritance and Marriage in a North Norwegian Fjord." *Folk,* 6: 35-45.

Brush, S. B. (1975). "The Concept of Carrying Capacity for Systems of Shifting Cultivation." *American Anthropologist,* 77: 799-811.

Burnahm, P., and R. F. Ellen, eds. (1979). *Social and Ecological Systems.* New York: Academic Press.

Caldwell, J. C. (1975). "The Sahelian Drought and Its Demographic Implications." Overseas Liaison Committee Paper No. 8. Washington: American Council on Education.

Carniero, R. L. (1960). "Slash-and-Burn Agriculture: A Closer Look at Its Implications for Settlement Patterns." In A. F. C. Wallace, ed., *Men and Cultures.* Philadelphia: University of Pennsylvania Press.

Carniero, R. (1961). "Slash-and-Burn Cultivation among the Kuikuru and Its Implications for Cultural Development in the Amazon Basin." *Anthropologica,* Supplement No. 2, pp. 47-67.

Chen, L. C., S. Ahmed, and W. H. Mosley (1974). "A Prospective Study of Birth Interval Dynamics in Rural Bangladesh." *Population Studies,* 28: 277-297.

Childe, V. G. (1951). *Man Makes Himself.* New York: New American Library.

Chubb, L. (1961). *Ibo Land Tenure.* Ibadan: Ibadan University Press.

Clarke, W. C. (1966). "From Extensive to Intensive Shifting Cultivation: a Succession from New Guinea." *Ethnology,* 5: 347-359.

Clarke, W. C. (1976). "Maintenance of Agriculture and Human Habitats within a Tropical Forest Ecosystem." *Human Ecology,* 4: 247-259.

Codere, H. (1950). *Fighting with Property.* New York: Augustin.

Codere, H. (1956). "The Amiable Side of Kwakiutl Life." *American Anthropologist,* 58: 334-351.

Cohen, Y., ed. (1968). *Man in Adaptation: The Cultural Present.* Chicago: Aldine.

Cole, J. W. (1969). "Economic Alternatives in the Upper Nonsberg." *Anthropological Quarterly,* 42: 186-213.

Cole, J. W. (1970). "Inheritance Processes and Their Social Consequences: A Case Study from Northern Italy." *Sociologica: rivista di studi sociali,* 4(N.S.): 133-146.

Conklin, H. C. (1954). "Shifting Cultivation." *Annals of the New York Academy of Sciences,* 17: 133-142.

Conklin, H. C. (1957). "Hanunóo Agriculture." FAO Forestry Development Paper No. 12. Rome: Food and Agriculture Organization of the United Nations.

Conklin, H. C. (1961). "Study of Shifting Cultivation." *Current Anthropology,* 2: 27-61.

Conklin, H. C. (1980). *Ethnographic Atlas of Ifugao: A Study of Environment, Culture, and Society in Northern Luzon.* New Haven: Yale University Press.

Conklin, H. C. (1974). "Ethnographic Research in Ifugao." In E. V. Vogt, ed., *Aerial Photography in Anthropological Field Work.* Cambridge: Harvard University Press. Pp. 140-159.

Cowgill, G. L. (1975). "On Causes and Consequences of Ancient and Modern Population Changes." *American Anthropologist,* 77: 505-525.

Curtin, P. (1964). *The Image of Africa.* Madison: University of Wisconsin Press.

Dahl, G., and A. Hjort (1976). *Having Herds: Pastoral Herd Growth and Household Economy.* Stockholm Studies in Social Anthropology #2. Stockholm: Department of Social Anthropology, University of Stockholm.

Daly, M., and M. Wilson (1978). *Sex, Evolution, and Behavior.* North Scituate, Mass.: Duxbury.

Damas, D. (1969a). "Environment, History, and Central Eskimo Society." In D. Damas, ed., *Ecological Essays.* Ottawa: National Museum of Canada, Bulletin No. 230. Pp. 40-64.

Damas, D. (1969b). "The Study of Cultural Ecology and the Ecology Conference." In D. Damas, ed., *Ecological Essays.* Ottawa: National Museum of Canada, Bulletin No. 230. Pp. 1-12.

de Laguna, F. (1972). *Under Mount Saint Elias: The History and Culture of the Yakutat Tlingit.* Smithsonian Contributions to Anthropology, vol. 7. Washington: Smithsonian Institution.

Demeny, P. (1974). "The Populations of the Underdeveloped Countries." *Scientific American,* 231(3): 148-159.

Deshler, W. (1963). "Cattle in Africa: Distribution, Types, and Problems." *Geographical Review,* 53: 52-58.

Deshler, W. (1965). "Native Cattle Keeping in Eastern Africa." In A. Leeds and A. P. Vayda, eds., *Man, Culture, and Animals.* Washington, D.C.: American Association for the Advancement of Science. Pp. 153-168.

de Schlippe, P. (1956). *Shifting Cultivation in Africa: The Zande System of Agriculture.* London: Routledge and Kegan Paul.

Donald, L., and D. H. Mitchell (1975). "Some Correlates of Local Group Rank among the Southern Kwakiutl." *Ethnology* 14: 325-346.

Drucker, P. (1939). "Land, Wealth, and Kinship in Northwest Coast Society." *American Anthropologist,* 41: 55-64.

Drucker, P. (1963). *Indians of the Northwest Coast.* New York: Natural History Press.

Drucker, P., and R. F. Heizer (1967). *To Make My Name Good.* Berkeley and Los Angeles: University of California Press.

Dumond, D. E. (1965). "Population Growth and Cultural Change." *Southwestern Journal of Anthropology,* 21: 302-324.

Dumond, D. E. (1972). "Population Growth and Political Centralization." In B. Spooner, ed., *Population Growth: Anthropological Implications.* Cambridge: MIT Press. Pp. 286-310.

Dyson-Hudson, R. (1972). "Pastoralism: Self Image and Behavioral Reality." In W. Irons and N. Dyson-Hudson, eds., *Perspectives on Nomadism.* Leiden: Brill. Pp. 30-47.

Dyson-Hudson, R., and N. Dyson-Hudson (1969). "Subsistence Herding in Uganda." *Scientific American,* 220: 76-89.

Dyson-Hudson, R., and E. A. Smith (1978). "Human Territoriality: An Ecological Reassessment." *American Anthropologist* 80:21-41.

Edgerton, R. B. (1965). " 'Cultural' vs. 'Ecological' Factors in the Expression of Values, Attitudes, and Personality Characteristics." *American Anthropologist,* 67: 442-447.

Ellen, R. (1982). *Environment, Subsistence and System: The Ecology of Small-Scale Social Formations.* Cambridge: Cambridge University Press.

Evans-Pritchard, E. E. (1940). *The Nuer.* London: Oxford University Press.

Evans-Pritchard, E. E. (1951). *Kinship and Marriage among the Nuer.* London: Oxford University Press.

Flannery, K. V. (1968). "Archeological Systems Theory and Early Mesoamerica." In B. J. Meggers, ed., *Anthropological Archeology in the Americas.* Washington: Anthropological Society of Washington. Pp. 67-87.

Forde, C. D. (1963). *Habitat, Economy and Society.* New York: Dutton. (First published 1934).

Fortes, M. (1957). "The Structure of Unilineal Descent Groups." *American Anthropologist,* 55: 17-41.

Freeman, J. D. (1955). *Iban Agriculture.* London: Her Majesty's Stationery Office.

Freilich, M. (1963). "The Natural Experiment, Ecology and Culture." *Southwestern Journal of Anthropology,* 19: 21-39.

Frisch, R. E. (1975). "Demographic Implications of the Biological Determinants of Female Fertility." *Social Biology,* 22: 17-22.

Geertz, C. (1963). *Agricultural Involution: The Processes of Ecological Change in Indonesia.* Berkeley and Los Angeles: University of California Press.

Gladwin, T. (1957). "Personality Structure in the Plains." *Anthropological Quarterly,* 30: 111-124.

Gleave, M. B., and H. P. White (1969). "Population Density and Agricultural Systems in West Africa." In M. F. Thomas and G. W. Whittington, eds., *Environment and Land Use in Africa.* London: Methuen. Pp. 273-300.

Glickman, M. (1971). "Kinship and Credit among the Nuer." *Africa,* 41: 306-319.

Goldschmidt, W. (1965). "Theory and Strategy in the Study of Cultural Adaptability." *American Anthropologist,* 67: 402-407.

Gourou, P. (1966). *The Tropical World.* 4th ed. New York: Wiley.

Gray, R. F. (1964). "Introduction." In R. F. Gray and P. H. Gulliver, eds., *The Family Estate in Africa.* London: Routledge and Kegan Paul. Pp. 1-6.

Grigg, D. B. (1979). "Ester Boserup's Theory of Agrarian Change: A Critical Review." *Progress in Human Geography* 3:64-68.

Gross, D. R. (1975). "Protein Capture and Cultural Development in the Amazon Basin." *American Anthropologist,* 77: 526-549.

Gross, D. R. (1984). "Ecosystems and Methodological Problems in Ecological Anthropology." In E. F. Moran, ed., *The Ecosystem Concept in Anthropology.* Boulder, CO: Westview. Pp. 253-263.

Grossman, L. S. (1981). "The Cultural Ecology of Economic Development." *Annals of the Association of American Geographers* 71:220-236.

Grossman, L. S. (1984). *Peasants, Subsistence Ecology, and Development in the Highlands of Papua, New Guinea.* Princeton: Princeton University Press.

Guemple, D. L. (1965). "Saunik: Name Sharing as a Factor Governing Eskimo Kinship Terms." *Ethnology,* 4: 323-335.

Gulliver, P. H. (1955). *The Family Herds.* London: Routledge and Kegan Paul.

Haaland, G. (1977). "Pastoral Systems of Production: the Socio-Cultural Context and Some Economic and Ecological Implications." In P. O'Keefe and B. Wisner, eds., *Landuse and Development.* London: International African Institute, Pp. 179-193.

Hallowell, A. I. (1949). "The Size of Algonkian Hunting Territories: A Function of Ecological Adjustment." *American Anthropologist,* 51: 35-45.

Hanks, L. M. (1972). *Rice and Man: Agricultural Ecology in Southeast Asia.* Chicago: Aldine.

Hardesty, D. C. (1977). *Ecological Anthropology.* New York: Wiley.

Hardin, G. (1968). "The Tragedy of the Commons." *Science,* 162: 1243-1248.

Harrell, B. B. (1981). "Lactation and Menstruation in Cultural Perspective." *American Anthropologist* 83:796-823.

Harris, D. R. (1972). "Swidden Systems and Settlement." In P. J. Ucko, R. Tringham, and G. W. Dimbleby, eds., *Man, Settlement, and Urbanism.* London: Duckworth.

Harris, M. (1969). "Monistic Determinism: Anti-Service." *Southwestern Journal of Anthropology* 25:198-206.

Harris, M. (1974). *Cows, Pigs, Wars, and Witches.* New York: Vintage Books.

Harris, M. (1977). *Cannibals and Kings: The Origins of Cultures.* New York: Vintage Books.

Hayden, B. (1975). "The Carrying Capacity Dilemma." In A. C. Swedlund, ed., *Population Studies in Archaeology and Biological Anthropology.* Memoir 30, pp. 11-21. Washington, D.C.: Society for American Archaeology.

Helm, J. (1962). "The Ecological Approach in Anthropology." *American Journal of Sociology,* 67: 630-639.

Helm, J. (1968). "The Nature of Dogrib Socioterritorial Groups." In R. B. Lee and I. DeVore, eds., *Man the Hunter.* Chicago: Aldine. Pp. 118-125.

Herskovits, M. J. (1924). "A Preliminary Consideration of the Culture Areas of Africa." *American Anthropologist,* 26: 50-63.

Herskovits, M. J. (1926). "The Cattle Complex in East Africa." *American Anthropologist,* 28: 230-272, 361-388, 494-528.

Herskovits, M. J. (1965). *Economic Anthropology.* New York: Norton.

Howell, N. (1976). "Toward a Uniformitarian Theory of Human Paleodemography." *Journal of Human Evolution,* 5: 25-40.

Howell, N. (1979). *Demography of the Dobe Area !Kung.* New York: Academic Press.

Hunter, J. M. (1966). "Ascertaining Population Carrying Capacity under Traditional Systems of Agriculture in Developing Countries." *Professional Geographer,* 18: 151-54.

Hunter, J. M. (1967). "Population Pressure in a Part of the West African Savanna: A Study of Nangodi, Northeast Ghana." *Annals of the Association of American Geographers,* 57: 101-114.

Huntington, E. (1963). *The Human Habitat.* New York: Norton.

Igbozurike, M. U. (1971). "Against Monoculture." *Professional Geographer,* 23: 113-117.

Jacobs, A. H. (1965). "African Pastoralists: Some General Remarks." *Anthropological Quarterly,* 38: 144-154.

Jain, A. K., et al. (1970). "Demographic Aspects of Lactation and Postpartum Amenorrhea." *Demography,* 7: 255-271.

Jochim, M. A. (1981). *Strategies for Survival: Cultural Behavior in an Ecological Context.* New York: Academic Press.

Johnson, A. (1975). "Time Allocation in a Machiguenga Community." *Ethnology,* 14: 301-310.

Knight, Rolf (1965). "A Re-examination of Hunting, Trapping, and Territoriality among the Northeastern Algonkian Indians." In A. Leeds and A. P. Vayda, eds., *Man, Culture, and Animals.* Washington, D.C.: American Association for the Advancement of Science. Pp. 27-42.

Kolata, G. B. (1974). "!Kung Hunter-Gatherers: Feminism, Diet, and Birth Control." *Science,* 185: 932-934.

Konner, M., and C. Worthman (1980). "Nursing Frequency, Gonadal Function, and Birth Spacing among !Kung Hunter-Gatherers." *Science* 207:788-791.

Kroeber, A. L. (1923). *Anthropology.* New York: Harcourt.

Kroeber, A. L. (1939). *Cultural and Natural Areas of North America.* Berkeley: University of California Press.

Ladejinsky, W. (1969). "The Green Revolution in Bihar—The Kosi Area: A Field Trip." *Economic and Political Weekly,* Vol. 4, No. 39, September 27, 1969. Reprinted in Agricultural Development Council Reprint No. 28. New York: Agricultural Development Council.

Lagemann, J. (1977). *Traditional African Farming Systems in Eastern Nigeria.* Munich: Weltforum Verlag.

Leacock, E. (1954). "The Montagnais Hunting Territory and the Fur Trade." American Anthropological Association Memoir 78, Vol. 56, No. 5, Part 2.

Leaf, M. J. (1972). *Information and Behavior in a Sikh Village.* Berkeley: University of California Press.

Leaf, M. J. (1984). *Song of Hope: The Green Revolution in a Panjab Village.* New Brunswick, NJ: Rutgers University Press.

Lee, R. B. (1968). "What Hunters Do for a Living, or How to Make out on Scarce Resources." In R. B. Lee and I. DeVore, eds., *Man the Hunter.* Chicago: Aldine. Pp. 30-48.

Lee, R. B. (1969). "!Kung Bushman Subsistence: An Input-Output Analysis." In D. Damas, ed., *Ecological Essays.* Ottawa: National Museum of Canada, Bulletin No. 230. Pp. 73-94.

Lee, R. B. (1972a). "The Shift to Sedentary Living and Population Growth among the !Kung Bushmen." In B. Spooner, ed., *Population Growth: Anthropological Implications.* Cambridge: MIT Press. Pp. 329-342.

Lee, R. B. (1972b). "The Intensification of Social Life among the !Kung Bushmen." In B. Spooner, ed., *Population Growth: Anthropological Implications.* Cambridge: MIT Press. Pp. 343-350.

Lee, R. B. (1973). "Mongongo: The Ethnography of a Major Wild Food Resource." *Ecology of Food and Nutrition,* 2: 307-321.

Lee, R. B. (1979). *The !Kung San: Men, Women, and Work in a Foraging Society.* Cambridge: Cambridge University Press.

Lee, R. B., and I. DeVore, eds. (1968). *Man the Hunter.* Chicago: Aldine.

Lees, S. H., and D. G. Bates (1984). "Environmental Events and the Ecology of Cumulative Change." In E. F. Moran, ed., *the Ecosystem Concept in Anthropology.* Boulder, CO: Westview. Pp. 133-159.

Linares De Sapir, O. (1970). "Agriculture and Diola Society." In P. F. M. McLoughlin, ed., *African Food Production Systems: Cases and Theory.* Baltimore: Johns Hopkins Press.

Little, M. A., and G. E. B. Morren, Jr. (1976). *Ecology, Energetics, and Human Variability.* Dubuque, IA: Brown.

Manners, R. A. (1964). "Colonialism and Native Land Tenure: A Case Study in Ordained Accommodation." In R. A. Manners, ed., *Process and Pattern in Culture.* Chicago: Aldine. Pp. 266-280.

McLoughlin, P. F. M., ed. (1970). *African Food Production Systems: Cases and Theory.* Baltimore: Johns Hopkins Press.

Marshall, L. (1957). "The Kin Terminology System of the !Kung Bushmen." *Africa*, 27: 1-25.

Marshall, L. (1960). "!Kung Bushmen Bands." *Africa*, 30: 325-355.

Mauss, M., and M. Beuchat (1905). "Essai sur les variations saisonières des sociétés eskimos." *L'Année sociologique*, 9: 39-132.

Moerman, M. (1968). *Agricultural Change and Peasant Choice in a Thai Village*. Berkeley: University of California Press.

Moran, E. F. (1979). *Human Adaptibility: An Introduction to Ecological Anthropology*. North Scituate, MA: Duxbury.

Moran E. F. (1984). Limitations and Advances in Ecosystems Research. In E. F. Moran, ed., *The Ecosystem Concept in Anthropology*. Boulder, CO: Westview. Pp. 3-32.

Murdock, G. P. (1949). *Social Structure*. New York: Macmillan.

Nell, E. (1972). "Boserup and Intensity of Cultivation." *Peasant Studies Newsletter*, 1: 39-44.

Netting, R. McC. (1965). "A Trial Model of Cultural Ecology." *Anthropological Quarterly*, 38: 81-96.

Netting, R. McC. (1968). *Hill Farmers of Nigeria: Cultural Ecology of the Kofyar of the Jos Plateau*. Seattle: University of Washington Press.

Netting, R. McC. (1969a). "Do-It-Yourself Economic Surveys: Field Methods for Data Collection." *Rural Africana*, 8: 13-18.

Netting, R. McC. (1969b). "Ecosystems in Process: A Comparative Study of Change in Two West African Societies." In D. Damas, ed., *Ecological Essays*. Ottawa: National Museum of Canada, Bulletin No. 230. Pp. 102-112.

Netting, R. McC. (1973). "Fighting, Forest, and the Fly: Some Demographic Regulators among the Kofyar." *Journal of Anthropological Research*, 29: 164-179.

Netting, R. McC. (1974). "Agrarian Ecology." In B. J. Siegel, A. R. Beals, and S. A. Tyler, eds., *Annual Review of Anthropology*, Vol. 3. Palo Alto: Annual Reviews. Pp. 21-56.

Netting, R. McC. (1976). "What Alpine Peasants Have in Common: Observations on Communal Tenure in a Swiss Village." *Human Ecology*, 4: 135-146.

Netting R. McC. (1981). *Balancing on an Alp: Ecological Change and Continuity in a Swiss Mountain Community*. Cambridge: Cambridge University Press.

Netting, R. McC. (1982a). "Territory, Property, and Tenure." In R. McC. Adams, N. J. Smelser, and D. J. Treiman, eds., *Behavioral and Social Science Research: A National Resource*. Washington: National Academy Press. Pp. 446-502.

Netting, R. McC. (1982b). "The Ecological Perspective: Holism and Scholasticism in Anthropology." In E. A. Hoebel, R. Currier, S. Kaiser, eds., *Crisis in Anthropology*. New York: Garland. Pp. 271-292.

Netting R. McC. (1984). "Reflections on an Alpine Village as Ecosystem." In E. F. Moran, ed., *The Ecosystem Concept in Anthropology*. Boulder, CO: Westview. Pp. 225-235.

Nye, P. H., and D. J. Greenland (1950). "The Soil under Shifting Cultivation." Technical Communication No. 51. Harpenden, England: Commonwealth Bureau of Soils, Commonwealth Agricultural Bureau.

Oberg, K. (1973). *The Social Economy of the Tlingit Indians*. Seattle: University of Washington Press.

Odum, E. P. (1971). *Fundamentals of Ecology*. 3rd Edition. Philadelphia: Saunders.

Oliver, S. C. (1962). "Ecology and Cultural Continuity as Contributing Factors in the Social Organization of the Plains Indians." *University of California Publications in American Archaeology and Ethnology*, 48(1): 1-90.

Orans, M. (1975). "Domesticating the Functional Dragon: An Analysis of Piddocke's Potlatch." *American Anthropologist,* 77: 312-328.

Orlove, B. S. (1980). "Ecological Anthropology." *Annual Review of Anthropology* 9:235-273.

Palerm, A. (1955). "The Agricultural Basis of Urban Civilization in Mesoamerica." Reprinted in Y. Cohen, ed., *Man in Adaptation: The Cultural Present.* Chicago: Aldine.

Peterson, N. (1975). "Hunter Gatherer Territoriality: The Perspective from Australia." *American Anthropologist,* 77: 53-68.

Piddocke, S. (1965). "The Potlatch System of the Southern Kwakiutl: A New Perspective." *Southwestern Journal of Anthropology,* 21: 244-264.

Pimentel, D., et al. (1973). "Food Production and the Energy Crisis." *Science,* 182: 443-49.

Porter, P. W. (1965). "Environmental Potentials and Economic Opportunities." *American Anthropologist,* 67: 409-420.

Pospisil, L. (1963). *Kapauku Papuan Economy.* New Haven: Yale University Publications in Anthropology, No. 67.

Ralston, L. R. (n.d.). "The Potlatch and Northwest Coast Ecology." Unpublished student paper, Department of Anthropology, University of Pennsylvania.

Rappaport, R. A. (1967). *Pigs for the Ancestors: Ritual in the Ecology of a New Guinea People.* New Haven: Yale University Press.

Rappaport, R. A. (1969). "Some Suggestions Concerning Concept and Method in Ecological Anthropology." In D. Damas, ed., *Ecological Essays.* Ottawa: National Museum of Canada, Bulletin 230, pp. 184-188.

Rappaport, R. A. (1971a). "Nature, Culture, and Ecological Anthropology." In H. L. Shapiro, ed., *Man, Culture, and Society.* London: Oxford University Press. Pp. 237-267.

Rappaport, R. A. (1971b). "The Flow of Energy in an Agricultural Society." *Scientific American* 224(3):116-123.

Rawski, E. S. (1972). *Agricultural Change and the Peasant Economy of South China.* Cambridge: Harvard University Press.

Reining, C. C. (1966). *The Zande Scheme: An Anthropological Case Study of Economic Development in Africa.* Evanston: Northwestern University Press.

Richards, A. I. (1939). *Land, Labour and Diet in Northern Rhodesia.* London: Oxford University Press.

Richerson, P. J. (1977). "Ecology and Human Ecology: A Comparison of Theories in the Biological and Social Sciences." *American Ethnologist* 4:1-26.

Rosman, A., and P. Rubel (1971). *Feasting with Mine Enemy.* New York: Columbia University Press.

Sahlins, M. D. (1957). "Land Use and the Extended Family in Moala Fiji." *American Anthropologist,* 59: 449-462.

Sahlins, M. D. (1961). "The Segmentary Lineage: An Organization of Predatory Expansion." *American Anthropologist,* 63: 322-345.

Sahlins, M. D. (1964). "Culture and Environment: The Study of Cultural Ecology." In Sol Tax, ed., *Horizons in Anthropology.* Chicago: Aldine. Pp. 132-147.

Sahlins, M. D. (1972). *Stone Age Economics.* Chicago: Aldine.

Sahlins, M. (1976). *Culture and Practical Reason.* Chicago: University of Chicago Press.

Sanchez, P. A., D. E. Bandy, J. H. Villachica, J. J. Nicholaides (1982). "Amazon Basin Soils: Management for Continuous Crop Production." *Science* 216:821-827.

Sauer, C. O. (1963). *Land and Life.* Berkeley and Los Angeles: University of California Press.

Savishinsky, J. D. (1971). "Hare Indian Mobility and Stress." *American Anthropologist*, 73: 604-618.

Schneider, H. K. (1957). "The Subsistence Role of Cattle among the Pakot and in East Africa." *American Anthropologist*, 59: 278-300.

Schneider, H. K. (1970). *The Wahi Wanyaturu: Economics in an African Society.* Chicago: Aldine.

Schneider, H. K. (1974). "Economic Development and Economic Change: The Case of East African Cattle." *Current Anthropology*, 15: 259-276.

Schumacher, E. G. (1973). *Small Is Beautiful: Economics as if People Mattered.* New York: Harper and Row.

Scudder, T. (1962). *The Ecology of the Gwembe Tonga.* Manchester: Rhodes-Livingstone Institute.

Scudder, T., and E. Colson (1972). "The Kariba Dam Project: Resettlement and Local Initiative." In H. R. Bernard and P. Pelto, eds., *Technology and Social Change.* New York: Macmillan.

Service, E. R. (1966). *The Hunters.* Englewood Cliffs, N.J.: Prentice-Hall.

Shelford, V. E. (1963). *The Ecology of North America.* Urbana: University of Illinois Press.

Shepard, P. (1969). "Introduction: Ecology and Man—A Viewpoint." In P. Shepard and D. McKinley, eds., *The Subversive Science.* Boston: Houghton-Mifflin. Pp. 1-10.

Silberbauer, G. B. (1972). "The G/wi Bushmen." In M. G. Bicchieri, ed., *Hunters and Gatherers Today.* New York: Holt, Rinehart and Winston. Pp. 271-326.

Smith, E. A. (1984). "Anthropology, Evolutionary Ecology, and the Explanatory Limitations of the Ecosystem Concept." In E. F. Moran, ed., *The Ecosystem Concept in Anthropology.* Boulder, CO: Westview, Pp. 51-85.

Smith, P. E. L., and T. C. Young (1972). "The Evolution of Early Agriculture and Culture in Greater Mesopotamia: A Trial Model." In Brian Spooner, ed., *Population Growth: Anthropological Implications.* Cambridge: MIT Press. Pp. 1-59.

Solien de Gonzalez, N. M. (1964). "Lactation and Pregnancy: A Hypothesis." *American Anthropologist* 66:873-878.

Speck, F., and L. C. Eiseley (1939). "The Significance of the Hunting Territory Systems of the Algonkian in Social Theory." *American Anthropologist,* 41: 269-280.

Spencer, P. (1965). *The Samburu.* London: Routledge and Kegan Paul.

Spicer, E. H. (1952). *Human Problems in Technological Change.* New York: Russell Sage Foundation.

Spooner, B., ed. (1972). *Population Growth: Anthropological Implications.* Cambridge: MIT Press.

Spooner, B. (1973). *The Cultural Ecology of Pastoral Nomads.* Addison-Wesley Modules in Ahthropology, No. 45. Reading, Mass: Addison-Wesley.

Stenning, D. (1959). *Savannah Nomads.* London: Oxford University Press.

Steward, J. (1938). *Basin-Plateau Aboriginal Sociopolitical Groups.* Washington, D.C.: Bureau of American Ethnology, Bulletin 120.

Steward, J. (1955). *Theory of Culture Change.* Urbana: University of Illinois Press.

Steward, J. (1968). "Causal Factors and Processes in the Evolution of Pre-Farming Societies." In R. B. Lee and I. DeVore, eds., *Man the Hunter.* Chicago: Aldine. Pp. 321-334.

Stocking, G. (1968). *Race, Culture and Evolution: Essays in the History of Anthropology.* New York: Collier-Macmillan.

Stone, G. D., P. Johnson-Stone, and R. McC. Netting (1984). "Household Variability and Inequality in Kofyar Subsistence and Cash-Cropping Economies." *Journal of Anthropological Research* 40:90-108.

Suttles, W. (1962). "Variation in Habitat and Culture on the Northwest Coast." *Proceedings of the 34th International Congress of Americanists.* Horn-Vienna: Verlag Ferdinand Berger. Pp. 522-537.

Suttles, W. (1968). "Coping with Abundance." In R. B. Lee and I. DeVore, eds., *Man the Hunter.* Chicago: Aldine. Pp. 56-68.

Swift, J. (1977). "Sahelian Pastoralists: Underdevelopment, Desertification, and Famine." *Annual Review of Anthropology* 6:457-478.

Tatham, G. (1951). "Environmentalism and Possibilism." In G. Taylor ed., *Geography in the Twentieth Century.* New York: Philosophical Library.

Tax, S. (1953). *An Appraisal of Anthropology Today.* Chicago: University of Chicago Press.

Thomas, F. (1925). *The Environmental Basis of Society.* New York: Century.

Torry, W. I. (1984). "Social Science Research on Famine: A Critical Evaluation." *Human Ecology* 12:227-252.

Toynbee, A. J. (1947). *A Study of History.* Abridgment of Vols. I-VI by D. C. Somervell. New York: Oxford University Press.

Turnbull, C. M. (1965a). *The Forest People.* Garden City, N.Y.: Natural History Press.

Turnbull, C. M. (1965b). "The Mbuti Pygmies of the Congo." In J. L. Gibbs, Jr., ed., *Peoples of Africa.* New York: Holt, Rinehart and Winston. Pp. 281-317.

Turnbull, C. M. (1968). "The Importance of Flux in Two Hunting Societies." In R. B. Lee and I. DeVore, eds., *Man the Hunter.* Chicago: Aldine. Pp. 132-137.

Turnbull, C. M. (1982). *The Mbuti Pygmies: Change and Adaptation.* New York: Holt, Rinehart and Winston.

Turner, B. L., R. Q. Hanham, and A. V. Portararo (1977). "Population Pressure and Agricultural Intensity." *Annals of the Association of American Geographers* 67:384-396.

Udo, R. K. (1965). "Disintegration of Nucleated Settlement in East Nigeria." *Geographical Review,* 55: 53-67.

Vasey, D. E. (1979). "Population and Agricultural Intensity in the Humid Tropics." *Human Ecology* 7:269-302.

Vayda, A. P. (1968). "Hypotheses about Functions of War." In M. Fried, M. Harris, and R. Murphy, eds., *War: The Anthropology of Armed Conflict and Aggression.* Garden City: Natural History Press. Pp. 85-91.

Vayda, A. (1969). *Environment and Cultural Behavior.* Garden City, N.Y.: Natural History Press.

Vayda, A. (1971). "Phases of the Process of War and Peace among the Marings of New Guinea." *Oceania,* 42: 1-24.

Vayda, A. P., A. Leeds, and D. Smith (1961). "The Place of Pigs in Melanesian Subsistence." In *Proceedings of the American Ethnological Society.* Seattle: University of Washington Press.

Vayda, A. P., and R. A. Rappaport (1968). "Ecology, Cultural and Non-Cultural." In J. S. Clifton, ed., *Introduction to Cultural Anthropology.* Boston: Houghton-Mifflin. Pp. 477-497.

Vayda, A. P., and B. J. McCay (1975). "New Directions in Ecology and Ecological Anthropology." In B. J. Siegel, A. R. Beals, and S. A. Tyler, eds., *Annual Review of Anthropology,* Vol. 4. Palo Alto: Annual Reviews. Pp. 293-306.

Weinberg, D. (1965). "Models of Southern Kwakiutl Social Organization: General Systems." *Yearbook of the Society of General Systems Research,* 10: 169-181.

Wienpahl, J. (1984). *Livestock Production and Social Organization among the Turkana.* Ph.D. Dissertation, Department of Anthropology, University of Arizona.

Wilmsen, E. (1978). "Seasonal Effects of Dietary Intake on Kalahari San." *Federation of American Societies for Experimental Biology Proceedings* 37:25-32.

Winterhalder, B., and E. A. Smith, eds. (1981). *Hunter-Gatherer Foraging Strategies: Ethnographic and Archaeological Analyses.* Chicago: University of Chicago Press.

Wissler, C. (1926). *The Relation of Nature to Man in Aboriginal America.* New York: Oxford University Press.

Wolf, E. R. (1962). "Cultural Dissonance in the Italian Alps." *Comparative Studies in Society and History,* 5: 1-14.

Wolf, E. R. (1966). *Peasants.* Englewood Cliffs, N.J.: Prentice-Hall.

Woodburn, J. (1968). "An Introduction to Hadza Ecology." In R. B. Lee and I. DeVore, eds., *Man the Hunter.* Chicago: Aldine. Pp. 49-55.

Wynne-Edwards, V. C. (1965). "Self-Regulating Systems in Populations of Animals." *Science,* 147: 1543-1548.

INDEX